AF317051

DEMYSTIFYING PROMPT ENGINEERING

AI PROMPTS AT YOUR FINGERTIPS

A STEP-BY-STEP GUIDE

HARISH BHAT

ISBN: 979-8-9883791-0-2 (Paperback)
ISBN: 979-8-9883791-1-9 (Hardcover)

TABLE OF CONTENTS

About the Author

Over the past 25 years, I have had the privilege of being an integral part of the dynamic & disruptive technology industry in Silicon Valley. During this time, I have been dedicated to assisting customers in addressing their business needs through innovative technology-enabled solutions. Some of the key responsibilities handled by me include:

a) Leading a global business unit that delivers product engineering services to software product companies and emerging new businesses.

b) Assisting Fortune 500 customers with application modernization and application management services, to increase agility, enhance customer centricity, and improve operational efficiency.

c) Driving Go-to-Market initiatives in collaboration with leading application software and tools vendors to deliver integrated life cycle management solutions to customers.

d) Leading a software products company that provides IT management solutions to some of the world's leading banks, financial processors, retailer and independent deployers of smart kiosks, checkout systems and cash dispensers.

e) Incubating and running a Managed Services business, delivering intelligent cloud-based infrastructure management services to banks and credit unions.

Throughout my extensive customer engagements in the US, I have witnessed the incredible impact of disruptive technologies. AI-enabled workflows have rapidly proliferated in the enterprise. Today, with the introduction of generative AI Chatbots like ChatGPT, we stand on the cusp of the AI revolution. It is rapidly transforming businesses and redefining career roles. The future is rolling in faster than we had ever imagined, and while the stakes are high, the opportunities on the horizon are profound.

Embedding AI is now on the agenda of every boardroom. I strongly believe that every professional needs to enhance their skills to thrive and grow in the AI-enabled enterprise. AI skills like Prompt Engineering are set to become essential requirements for every professional. This book, "Demystifying Prompt Engineering," is my passionate endeavor to help you build AI readiness and fast-track your career in this transformative era.

In addition to the book, I have created a companion website, **www.getAIready.com,** where I will be regularly sharing insights and updates on the topic of prompt engineering. I encourage you to visit the website regularly to dive deeper into the subject and stay updated.

Harish Bhat
California, USA
harish@getAIready.com

INTRODUCTION

Generative AI tools, like ChatGPT, are transforming industries and accelerating innovation. With the ability to rapidly deliver insights, generate content, analyze sentiment, and even perform financial analysis, companies are adopting these tools to automate mundane tasks, streamline workflows, and enhance customer service.

A recent study done by Resume Builder found that 91% of employers prefer workers with experience in AI tools. The ability to use these AI tools is now valued more than computer programming by many firms, according to the World Economic Form. A year-long study by Stanford University and MIT shows that generative AI tools increased customer service worker productivity by 14% on average in a Fortune 500 software firm.

Every professional in every industry will be impacted by AI in the workplace. Learn the skills needed to harness the power of the tool in your workday and transform your business.

This rapid adoption has created a new and highly creative role: the Prompt Engineer. What exactly does a Prompt Engineer do?

A Rubik's cube is a good analogy for the role of a prompt engineer; both require careful and precise manipulation to achieve the desired outcome. Just as a Rubik's cube has a specific set of algorithms that need to be followed to solve it, a prompt engineer needs to carefully select and combine the right words, phrases, and inputs to create the desired output from the AI model.

Moreover, solving a Rubik's cube requires a deep understanding of the cube's structure, just as a prompt engineer must have a strong understanding of the AI model they are working with. Both tasks require critical thinking, problem-solving skills, and the ability to work methodically towards a specific goal.

Like solving a Rubik's cube, prompt engineering is an iterative process. A prompt engineer must continually fine-tune and adjust the inputs to optimize the output, just as a Rubik's cube solver must continually adjust the cube to align the colors.

The Rubik's cube analogy captures the complexity, precision, and iterative nature of prompt engineering, making it a fitting comparison for the role of a prompt engineer.

Solving a Rubik's cube takes great skill, and so does writing effective prompts. That is why I have written *Demystifying Prompt Engineering*, a step-by-step guide to help you master the foundation attributes of prompt engineering. Learn the AI Prompting skills to communicate with your AI Models like ChatGPT.

Imagine the possibilities:

- A high school teacher in Philadelphia using ChatGPT to grade essays and then teach students how to improve their writing skills.

- A content marketer using ChatGPT to research trending topics, write engaging content, and optimize it for search engines.

- A product manager using ChatGPT to research market requirements and do competitive analysis for a new sports watch.

- An HR manager using ChatGPT to analyze employee engagement survey results and gain insights for retention programs.

These are not futuristic dreams, but realities made possible by generative AI tools today. Professionals who master the skills of communicating with AI models will be richly rewarded by the growing digital economy.

Demystifying Prompt Engineering is the ultimate guide to unleashing the power of ChatGPT. I authored this book with ChatGPT as my Co-pilot. Master the foundational attributes of prompt engineering, dive into advanced topics, and learn best practices from industry experts.

Hone your skills in writing effective AI prompts with our hands-on labs and ready-to-use prompt cookbooks. Learn how to leverage the power of ChatGPT to create engaging content, automate repetitive tasks, enhance customer service, and streamline workflows with ease. This step-by-step guide will help you hit the ground running in no time.

The Age of AI is upon us, and Prompt Engineering is the new literacy that every professional needs to embrace in order to harness the incredible power of machines. Master Prompt Engineering skills outlined in this book to unleash your creativity and productivity.

I am glad you are here.

Harish Bhat

CHAPTER 1

Introduction to ChatGPT

In this chapter, the topics covered include:

- ChatGPT Overview
- Large Language Models
- Output Formats of ChatGPT
- ChatGPT Use Cases
- Differences Between ChatGPT and Web Search

✎ What is ChatGPT?

Imagine having a virtual assistant that can help you with a wide range of tasks, from generating content for your website, to helping you come up with creative ideas, automating routine tasks or, even assisting you in making important decisions. ChatGPT is like a smart, witty, and resourceful genie in your pocket. It is always there to make your workday a little more magical and a lot more fun!

ChatGPT has a wide range of capabilities that can be leveraged across various industries and professions. Here is a brief overview of ChatGPT's key capabilities:

1. *Content Generation*: Generate text content for a variety of purposes, such as authoring articles, creating marketing copy, crafting product descriptions, generating social media posts, and more.

2. *Idea Generation*: Help spark creative ideas by generating text prompts, brainstorming concepts, and providing inspiration for content creation, product development, and problem-solving.

3. *Language Translation*: Assist with language translation tasks by generating translations from one language to another, making it useful for global communication and localization efforts.

4. *Data Analysis*: Analyze data by generating summaries, insights, and visualizations from large volumes of text, making it valuable for data-driven decision-making and analysis.

5. *Virtual Assistance*: Serve as a virtual assistant, providing information, answering questions, and helping with tasks like scheduling, reminders, and more.

6. *Summarization*: Provide summaries of long documents, articles, or reports, making it efficient for extracting key information and insights from voluminous text.

7. *Question Answering*: Provide accurate answers to questions based on the information provided in the prompts, making it useful for information retrieval and knowledge-based tasks.

8. *Code Generation*: Assist with generating code snippets, templates, and examples for programming tasks, making it helpful for developers and programmers.

9. *Conversation Simulation*: Simulate conversation scenarios, allowing users to engage in interactive conversations and practice dialogues for various purposes, such as customer service, sales, or training simulations.

10. *Personalization*: ChatGPT can be fine-tuned and customized with prompt engineering techniques to adapt to specific domains, industries, or user preferences, enabling personalized and tailored interactions.

These capabilities make ChatGPT a versatile and powerful tool for professionals across domains and industries, providing opportunities to streamline tasks, generate content, gain insights, and enhance communication.

This book will help you unleash the full potential of ChatGPT and leverage its capabilities to achieve your professional goals.

 Overview of Large Language Models

Large Language Models, like ChatGPT, are advanced artificial intelligence (AI) models that are capable of understanding and generating human-like text. These models are trained on massive amounts of data and have the ability to generate text that is coherent, contextually relevant, and grammatically accurate.

The key capabilities of Large Language Models like ChatGPT include:

1. *Language Generation*: Generate text based on prompts provided by users, making it useful for tasks such as content creation, writing assistance, and storytelling.

2. *Language Understanding*: Comprehend and analyze text provided in prompts, allowing it to extract key information, perform text classification, and answer questions.

3. *Contextual Adaptation*: Understand the context of the prompt and generate text, accordingly, making it capable of adapting to different writing styles, tones, and domains.

4. *Creative Text Generation*: Generate text that goes beyond simple rephrasing or copying of input prompts, making it capable of producing creative and original content.

5. *Interactive Conversations*: Engage in interactive conversations with users, allowing for dynamic exchanges that simulate human-like conversations.

These capabilities make Large Language Models like ChatGPT incredibly powerful and versatile for various professional use cases, such as content creation, copywriting, customer service, virtual assistance, and more.

By understanding the foundations of Prompt Engineering, you can effectively utilize the capabilities of Large Language Models and harness their potential to enhance your professional endeavors.

🖥️ Output Formats Generated by ChatGPT

ChatGPT can generate output in various formats to suit different needs. Here is a summary of the more common output formats:

1. *Text Response*: Generate text responses in a conversational format, simulating human-like conversations. These responses can be used for virtual customer service, chatbots, or other interactive conversational applications.

2. *Paragraph or Long-form Text*: Longer text outputs, such as paragraphs or articles, which can be used for content creation, article writing, or summarization tasks.

3. Bullets or Lists: Concise bulleted lists which can be used for creating outlines, summarizing information, or generating structured content.

4. *Code Snippets*: Create code snippets or programming examples, which can be used for coding assistance, code generation, or software development tasks.

5. *Summaries*: Summarized versions of longer text inputs, providing condensed and relevant information for quick overviews or summaries of content.

6. *Answers to Questions*: Direct answers to questions, making it useful for question-answering tasks, fact-checking, or information retrieval.

7. *Tables*: Generate tables, which can be used for presenting structured information, data visualization, or creating reports.

8. *Charts or Graphs*: Visual representations of data, such as charts or graphs, which can be used for data visualization, business intelligence, or analytics purposes.

9. *Infographics*: Generate visually appealing infographics, which can be used for presenting information in a visually engaging and informative manner.

10. *Dynamic or Interactive Content*: Generate dynamic or interactive content, such as interactive surveys, quizzes, or assessments, which can be used for engaging and interactive user experiences.

These output formats enable ChatGPT to generate a wide range of content, from structured data presentations to visually appealing infographics, templates, and interactive content. Understanding these capabilities can help you harness the power of ChatGPT in your Prompt Engineering efforts and create a diverse range of outputs to suit your specific requirements.

Use Cases of ChatGPT

Let us look at a day in the life of ChatGPT by mapping it to different user personas and roles across industry segments:

Content Developer:

- *Content Generation*: Use ChatGPT to generate blog posts, articles, social media content, and more.

- *Content Editing*: Utilize ChatGPT for proofreading, grammar checking, and improving writing quality.

- *Idea Generation*: Generate creative ideas and prompts for content creation using ChatGPT.

- *Topic Research*: Use ChatGPT to research and gather information on various topics for content development.

- *Headline Generation*: Generate catchy headlines and titles for articles and blog posts using ChatGPT.

Retailer:

- *Product Description Generation*: Use ChatGPT to generate compelling product descriptions for online listings.
- *Customer Support*: Utilize ChatGPT to provide quick responses and answers to customer inquiries.
- *Marketing Campaigns*: Generate marketing copy and promotional content using ChatGPT for online campaigns.
- *Product Naming*: Generate unique and catchy product names using ChatGPT to enhance brand identity.
- *Competitive Analysis*: Use ChatGPT to gather information and insights on competitors for strategic decision-making.

Product Manager:

- *Feature Ideas*: Generate ideas for new product features or improvements using ChatGPT.
- *User Feedback Analysis*: Utilize ChatGPT to analyze and extract insights from user feedback for product improvement.
- *Product Road Mapping*: Use ChatGPT to generate product roadmap plans and prioritize feature development.
- *Market Research*: Gather market research insights using ChatGPT for product positioning and market analysis.
- *Customer Segmentation*: Use ChatGPT to analyze data and segment customers for targeted product offerings.

Marketing Manager:

- *Content Planning*: Use ChatGPT to generate content ideas, plan content calendars, and schedule social media posts.
- *Copywriting*: Generate compelling ad copy, email subject lines, and social media captions using ChatGPT.
- *Audience Targeting*: Utilize ChatGPT to generate audience profiles and target specific segments for marketing campaigns.

- *Campaign Optimization*: Use ChatGPT to analyze campaign performance data and generate optimization recommendations.
- *Brand Messaging*: Generate consistent and cohesive brand messaging using ChatGPT for marketing materials.

Small Business Owner:

- *Social Media Management*: Use ChatGPT to schedule social media posts, generate captions, and manage social media content.
- *Customer Engagement*: Utilize ChatGPT to respond to customer inquiries, provide quick support, and engage with customers.
- *Content Creation*: Generate blog posts, website content, and promotional materials using ChatGPT for small business marketing.
- *Email Marketing*: Generate compelling email content, subject lines, and CTAs using ChatGPT for effective email campaigns.
- *Online Advertising*: Generate ad copy, headlines, and call-to-action using ChatGPT for online advertising campaigns.

Human Resources:

- *Employee Onboarding*: Use ChatGPT to generate onboarding materials, training resources, and orientation guides for new employees.
- *Employee Communications*: Utilize ChatGPT to generate HR-related announcements, memos, and policies for internal communications.
- *Performance Reviews*: Use ChatGPT to generate performance review templates, feedback forms, and self-assessment prompts for employees.

- *Employee Surveys:* Generate employee survey questions, feed-back forms, and polls using ChatGPT for gathering insights and feedback.

- *Employee Handbook:* Use ChatGPT to generate or update employee handbooks with relevant policies, procedures, and guidelines.

Differences Between ChatGPT and Web Search

We are all familiar with web search functions provided by search engines like Google and Bing. Unlike traditional search engines, ChatGPT does not go to the internet to serve a search request with a bunch of links, which at times may have no relevance to your search query. It is different from traditional web search in several ways:

- *Interaction:* ChatGPT allows for interactive conversations where users can have dynamic exchanges with the model, similar to a conversation with a human, whereas traditional web search is typically a one-way interaction where users input keywords and receive search results.

- *Contextual Understanding:* ChatGPT is designed to understand and respond to the context of the conversation, considering the previous messages and context provided by the user, which allows for more personalized and relevant responses. In traditional web search, the search engine does not maintain context and relies solely on the input query to generate results.

- *Natural Language Processing:* ChatGPT is designed to process and generate human-like responses in natural language, making it easier for users to have conversational interactions. Traditional web search cannot process and interpret queries in natural language as effectively, mainly due to the lack of context and increased focus on the keywords of the query to fetch search results. Also, the results retrieved may not always be in natural language.

- *Customization*: ChatGPT can be fine-tuned and customized for specific tasks or domains, allowing it to provide more specialized and tailored responses based on the specific use case. Traditional web search is more generic and often offers little to no means of personalization to suit specific business/user needs.

- *Contextual Generation*: ChatGPT has the ability to generate text-based responses, which can be useful for tasks such as content creation, writing assistance, and more. Traditional web search primarily provides links to existing web content, without the ability to generate text-based responses.

Overall, ChatGPT provides a more interactive, conversational, and context-aware experience compared to traditional web search, making it well-suited for tasks that require dynamic conversations and personalized responses.

◎ Chapter Summary

- ChatGPT is a Large Language Model powered by AI that can generate human-like text responses based on prompts provided by users.

- ChatGPT has a wide range of capabilities, including content generation, idea generation, language translation, data analysis, virtual assistance, summarization, question answering, code generation, conversation simulation, and personalization.

- Large Language Models like ChatGPT are advanced AI models capable of generating coherent, contextually relevant, and grammatically accurate text.

- Output formats generated by ChatGPT include text responses, paragraphs or long-form text, bullets or lists, code snippets, summaries, and answers to questions.

- Understanding the differences between ChatGPT and web search is crucial for leveraging ChatGPT effectively.
- Monetizing ChatGPT can be done through various avenues such as content creation, copywriting, virtual customer service, and more.

CHAPTER 2

Introduction to Prompt Engineering

In this chapter, we cover:

- Definition of Prompt Engineering
- Importance of Prompt Engineering in AI Communications
- Overview of Different Types of Prompts
- Foundations of Prompt Engineering
- Progressive Experimentation with ChatGPT

🖌 Definition of Prompt Engineering

Prompt Engineering is the art of crafting clear and precise instructions that guide language models like GPT-3 to generate accurate and meaningful responses. It is like being the captain of a ship, steering the model towards the desired outcomes. It empowers you to communicate effectively with the model by providing context, relevance, and clarity to your prompts.

Just like giving directions to a friend, a well-crafted prompt provides the necessary details, sets the right tone, and specifies the desired output. It is like a recipe that guides the model in generating responses that meet your expectations. From creating reports and blog posts to designing logos and sales proposals, prompt engineering ensures that the model understands your requirements and delivers the results you need.

Think of prompt engineering as your co-pilot, helping you to enhance creativity, accelerate productivity, gain data-driven insights, and deliver enhanced customer service. By mastering the basics of prompt engineering, you can unleash the full potential of AI language models and embark on an exciting journey of creative possibilities.

Importance of Prompt Engineering in AI Communications

Imagine having a conversation with an AI that perfectly understands your needs, generates accurate responses, and delivers exactly what you are looking for. That is the power of prompt engineering in AI communication! As AI becomes increasingly prevalent in our daily lives, effective prompt engineering plays a critical role in enabling seamless interactions between humans and machines.

The importance of prompt engineering lies in its ability to bridge the gap between human intent and machine understanding. With the right prompts, you can guide the AI engine to produce contextually relevant, coherent, and accurate responses. It empowers you to communicate your requirements in a way that the model can comprehend, resulting in meaningful and actionable outcomes.

Prompt engineering is not just about technical expertise, but also about effective communication. It helps in conveying the desired context, tone, and specificity in prompts, which are essential for obtaining the desired results. Whether it is designing a logo, drafting an email, or analyzing data, prompt engineering ensures that the AI understands your intent and delivers responses that meet your expectations.

By mastering prompt engineering, you can enhance productivity, glean valuable insights, and create personalized experiences with AI. It empowers you to harness the full potential of language models, making them powerful tools in various domains, such as customer service, content creation, and decision-making. So, embrace the importance of prompt engineering in AI communication and unlock new possibilities in your interactions with artificial intelligence!

Overview of Different Types of Prompts Used in Prompt Engineering

Here is an overview of the different types of prompts used in prompt engineering:

1. **Zero-Shot Prompts**: Zero-shot prompts allow a model to generate responses for tasks for which they were not explicitly trained. For example, a language model can be trained on a dataset for text generation but can also generate responses for tasks like question-answering or translation without being explicitly trained for those tasks. A zero-shot prompt typically includes a description of the desired task along with any necessary context or instructions.

   Example: *"Translate the following English text to French: {text}"*

2. **Chain-of-Thought Prompts**: Chain-of-thought prompts are used to guide a model to generate a series of coherent responses in a conversational manner. In this approach the model response is instructed to proceed step-by-step and present all the steps involved. Doing so reduces the possibility of inaccuracy of outcomes and makes assessing the model response easier.

System Message	User	Assistant
You are an AI assistant that helps people find information.	*Who was the most decorated (maximum medals) individual athlete in the Olympic games that were held in Sydney? Take a step-by-step approach in your response, cite sources, and give reasoning before sharing final answer in the below format: ANSWER is: <name>*	Step 1: Determine the year of the Sydney Olympic games. The Sydney Olympic games were held in the year 2000. Step 2: Find a list of individual athletes who won multiple medals in the 2000 Sydney Olympics. According to the official website of the Olympic Games, there were several individual athletes who won multiple medals in the 2000 Sydney Olympics. Some of the notable names include: • Ian Thorpe (Australia) - 3 gold, 2 silver, 0 bronze • Pieter van den Hoogenband (Netherlands) - 2 gold, 0 silver, 2 bronze • Lenny Krayzelburg (USA) - 3 gold, 0 silver, 0 bronze • Inge de Bruijn (Netherlands) - 3 gold, 1 silver, 0 bronze Step 3: Determine the athlete with the most medals. After reviewing the list of individual athletes who won multiple medals in the 2000 Sydney Olympics, we can see that the athlete with the most medals is Ian Thorpe from Australia, who won a total of 5 medals (3 gold and 2 silver). Therefore, the ANSWER is: Ian Thorpe.

3. **Instruction-Based Prompts**: Instruction-based prompts provide explicit instructions to guide the model's behavior. These prompts are designed to provide specific guidance or constraints on how the model should generate responses. Instructions can include information on tone, style, format, or other desired characteristics of the output.

Example: *"Write a persuasive email to promote a new product launch. Use a professional and enthusiastic tone, highlight the unique features of the product, and provide a clear call-to-action for customers to make a purchase."*

4. **Context-Based Prompts**: Context-based prompts provide contextual information to the model to guide its responses. These prompts typically include relevant information or context related to the task or topic to ensure the model generates accurate and coherent responses based on the provided context.

   Example: *"You are a weather forecast bot. Provide the current weather conditions for {city} including temperature, humidity, and wind speed."*

5. **Fill-in-the-Blank Prompts**: Fill-in-the-blank prompts are used to complete sentences or phrases provided by the user. These prompts typically include a placeholder or blank space that the model is expected to fill with the appropriate information or response.

   Example: *"Complete the following sentence: 'The best way to optimize website performance is by __________.'"*

Each type of prompt serves a different purpose in guiding the model's responses and can be used in various applications of prompt engineering to achieve desired outcomes.

⚙️ Understanding the Foundation of Prompt Engineering

Let us take a close look at five key attributes of effective prompts:

1. **Clarity**: An unambiguous prompt ensures that the model understands your intent correctly.

   Sample Prompt: *"Write a short story about a journey to the moon."*

   Comment: The prompt clearly specifies the desired outcome, providing clear instructions to the model.

2. **Context**: Providing relevant context in your prompt helps the model understand the context of your request.

   Sample Prompt: *"Translate the following English text to French: 'Hello, how are you?'"*

   Comment: The prompt presents the context of translating English to French and the specific text to be translated, providing the necessary context for the model to generate an accurate translation.

3. **Precision**: Keep your prompts concise and to the point. That helps the model focus on relevant information.

   Sample Prompt: *"Summarize the main points of the article on climate change."*

   Comment: The prompt conveys the desired outcome without unnecessary details, making it concise and effective.

4. **Specificity**: Specific prompts help in generating precise outputs aligned with your requirements.

   Sample Prompt: *"Design a logo for a children's toy company with bright colors and playful elements."*

   Comment: The prompt provides specific details about the desired logo, guiding the model to generate a logo that meets the specified criteria.

5. **Experimentation**: Prompt Engineering is an iterative process that involves experimentation and fine-tuning to achieve desired results. Do not be afraid to experiment with different prompts and iterate to improve the outcomes.

By crafting clear, context-rich, concise, specific, and experimental prompts, you can effectively communicate with AI models and generate amazing outputs aligned with your creative vision. In the next chapter, we will take a deep dive into the above five key attributes of effective prompts with specific examples and lab workouts.

🔧 Power Up Your Prompts With Effective Verbs

The use of strong verbs in writing prompts is essential for effective communication. These verbs give a clear direction to the user and make the prompt more actionable. Using weak verbs can lead to confusion and inaction.

Here are three examples of how strong verbs can make prompts more effective:

1. Weak: *"Can you tell me about your experience with our product?"*

    Strong: *"Describe how you felt while using our product."*

2. Weak: *"What are your thoughts on our website design?"*

    Strong: *"Evaluate the effectiveness of our website design in meeting your needs."*

3. Weak: *"Please provide feedback on our customer service."*

    Strong: *"Assess the quality of our customer service in resolving your issue."*

4. Weak: *"What do you think of our pricing strategy?"*

    Strong: *"Critique the effectiveness of our pricing strategy in relation to our competitors."*

5. Weak: *"Do you like our new feature?"*

    Strong: *"Evaluate the impact of our new feature on your overall experience with our product."*

Ten powerful verbs that can be used to write effective prompts for ChatGPT:

Explain	Analyze
Summarize	Evaluate
Predict	Identify
Compare	Clarify
Contrast	Define

Elevate Your Prompts with Nuances of Tone

Tone of voice refers to the attitude or feeling that is conveyed through language. In the context of effective prompts, the tone of voice used can have a significant impact on the success of the prompt. The tone of voice should be appropriate for the audience and the context, and should be designed to elicit the desired response.

Here are five examples of how tone of voice can be used in prompts:

1. Polite tone: *"Please provide the following information so that we can process your request quickly and efficiently."*

2. Assertive tone: *"Please complete the following steps to ensure that your account is set up correctly."*

3. Friendly tone: *"Hi there! We're so glad you're interested in our product. Please fill out the following form to get started."*

4. Urgent tone: *"We need your response as soon as possible in order to complete your order."*

5. Encouraging tone: *"You're almost there! Just one more step to complete your application and join our community."*

Ten powerful tone of voice ideas for effective prompts:

1. Clear and Direct: Use a straightforward tone to give a clear and direct message, without unnecessary words or phrases.

2. Friendly and Conversational: Use a friendly and conversational tone to make the user feel more comfortable and engaged.

3. Professional and Polite: Use a professional and polite tone to maintain a level of respect and formality in your prompt.

4. Empathetic and Understanding: Use an empathetic and understanding tone to show that you care about the user and their needs.

5. Excited and Enthusiastic: Use an excited and enthusiastic tone to create a sense of excitement and anticipation for the user.

6. Confident and Assuring: Use a confident and assuring tone to instill confidence in the user and let them know that they are in good hands.

7. Urgent and Actionable: Use an urgent and actionable tone to create a sense of urgency and encourage the user to take immediate action.

8. Concise and Informative: Use a concise and informative tone to provide the user with the information they need in a clear and concise manner.

9. Supportive and Encouraging: Use a supportive and encouraging tone to motivate the user and help them achieve their goals.

10. Playful and Fun: Use a playful and fun tone to add an element of fun and enjoyment to the user experience.

Progressive Experimentation for Refining Prompts

Progressive experimentation with ChatGPT involves an iterative and data-driven approach to refining prompts and optimizing the output of the language model for a specific use case or industry. It is about continuously experimenting and iterating to achieve desired results.

Here is an example of progressive experimentation with prompts using ChatGPT for generating product descriptions for a consumer goods company:

1. Initial Prompt: *"Generate a product description for a new organic shampoo."*

   Output: "Introducing our new organic shampoo - enriched with natural ingredients for healthy, shiny hair!"

2. Revised Prompt: *"Generate a product description for a new organic shampoo that promotes hair growth and prevents dandruff."*

   Output: "Experience the power of nature with our organic shampoo! 🌿 Enriched with nourishing ingredients, it promotes healthy hair growth, prevents dandruff, and leaves your locks feeling soft and silky."

3. Further Revised Prompt: *"Generate a product description for a new organic shampoo that promotes hair growth, prevents dandruff, and is free from harsh chemicals like sulfates and parabens."*

    Output: "Indulge in nature's goodness with our organic shampoo! 🌿 Formulated with botanical extracts, it promotes hair growth, prevents dandruff, and is free from sulfates, parabens, and other harmful chemicals for a truly natural and gentle hair care experience."

4. Experimenting with Product Benefits: *"Generate a product description for a new organic shampoo that promotes hair growth, prevents dandruff, is free from harsh chemicals, and adds volume to limp hair."*

    Output: "Elevate your hair care routine with our organic shampoo! 🌿 Boosting hair growth, preventing dandruff, and adding volume to limp locks, it is the ultimate choice for healthy and voluminous hair. Plus, it's free from harsh chemicals for a truly wholesome and revitalizing hair care experience."

5. Experimenting with Brand Messaging: *"Generate a product description for a new organic shampoo that promotes hair growth, prevents dandruff, is free from harsh chemicals, adds volume to limp hair, and is cruelty-free."*

    Output: "Join our movement towards natural and cruelty-free hair care with our organic shampoo! 🌿 With powerful ingredients that promote hair growth, prevent dandruff, add volume to limp locks, and are free from harsh chemicals, it's the perfect choice for conscious consumers who value the well-being of their hair and the environment."

Here is another example of progressive experimentation with prompts using ChatGPT for generating content for an electric automotive company:

1. Initial Prompt: *"Write a brief overview of our new electric vehicle model."*

   - The model generates a basic overview of the electric vehicle model, including general information about its specifications, performance, and features.

2. Iteration 1: *"Write a detailed description of our new electric vehicle model, emphasizing its long-range capability, fast charging technology, and eco-friendly features."*

   - The model is guided to highlight the long-range capability, fast charging technology, and eco-friendly features of the electric vehicle model, positioning it as an environment-friendly and convenient transportation option.

3. Iteration 2: *"Write a persuasive description of our new electric vehicle model, focusing on its cutting-edge design, advanced safety features, and smart connectivity options."*

   - The model is instructed to emphasize the cutting-edge design, advanced safety features, and smart connectivity options of the electric vehicle model, positioning it as a technologically advanced and safe choice for consumers.

4. Iteration 3: *"Write an engaging description of our new electric vehicle model, highlighting its exceptional performance, sporty handling, and exhilarating driving experience."*

   - The model is directed to emphasize the exceptional performance, sporty handling, and exhilarating driving experience of the electric vehicle model, positioning it as a high-performance and exciting option for driving enthusiasts.

5. Iteration 4: *"Write a customer-centric description of our new electric vehicle model, showcasing its spacious and comfortable interior, intuitive infotainment system, and advanced driver-assistance features."*

   - The model is prompted to focus on the customer-centric features of the electric vehicle model, including its spacious and comfortable interior, intuitive infotainment system, and advanced driver-assistance features, positioning it as a practical and user-friendly choice for everyday driving.

6. Final Prompt: *"Write a comprehensive description of our new electric vehicle model that combines all its unique features, including its long-range capability, fast charging technology, eco-friendly features, cutting-edge design, advanced safety features, smart connectivity options, exceptional performance, sporty handling, spacious and comfortable interior, intuitive infotainment system, and advanced driver-assistance features."*

   • The model is instructed to combine all the unique features of the electric vehicle model into a comprehensive and compelling description that highlights its overall value proposition.

Through progressive experimentation with prompts, you can tailor the product descriptions generated by ChatGPT to align with your brand messaging, highlight specific product benefits, and convey the unique value proposition of your product or service. Prompt Engineering enables you to iteratively optimize and customize the output from ChatGPT, providing you with an effective tool for generating compelling and persuasive product descriptions that resonate with your target audience.

Do You Need Programming Skills to Become a Prompt Engineer?

It helps to have some programming background, but you do not have to be a nerdy programmer to excel in Prompt Engineering. In fact, many of the successful prompt engineers have a background in languages or arts majors.

Prompt Engineering is more focused on creativity, critical thinking, and understanding the context and instructions needed to guide the language model. It involves skills such as crafting clear and specific prompts, experimenting with prompt variations, iterating through refinement, and optimizing the output based on the desired results.

These skills can be developed and honed through practice and experimentation, regardless of whether you have programming skills or not.

In the next chapter, dig deeper into the key attributes of prompt engineering with specific examples to help you get into the flow of Prompt Engineering.

◎ Chapter Summary

- The primary goal of Prompt Engineering is to craft clear and precise instructions to guide language models like GPT-3 for accurate and meaningful responses.

- Prompt Engineering is a crucial part of AI Communications to bridge the gap between human intent and machine understanding for seamless interactions between humans and machines.

- The different types of prompts are: zero-shot prompts, chain-of-thought prompts, instruction-based prompts, context-based prompts, and fill-in-the-blank prompts.

- Clarity, Relevance, Context, Format, and Constraints are the key attributes of effective prompts and make up the foundation of Prompt Engineering.

- Progressive experimentation with ChatGPT involves experimenting with different prompts, iterating and refining prompts, and learning from model outputs to improve prompt engineering skills.

- Prompt engineers are at the forefront of generative AI, crafting the instructions that fuel AI tools like ChatGPT, the industry's poster child. In many ways, the prompt engineer is akin to a skilled surgeon, guiding the AI in rewiring its neural pathways. Just as a surgeon uses precise techniques, the prompt engineer carefully designs prompts to shape the AI's output.

CHAPTER 3

Writing Effective Prompts

In this chapter, the topics covered include the 5 key attributes:

- Clarity
- Context
- Precision
- Sensitivity
- Creativity

Key Attributes of Good Prompt Writing

In this section let us examine some of the foundation attributes of prompts with specific examples.

1. **Clarity**: Effective prompts should be unambiguous, providing precise instructions to the language model. For example:

   - Unclear Prompt: *"Order pizza."*

     Clear Prompt: *"Generate a pizza order for a large Margherita pizza, thin crust, and extra cheese."*

2. **Context**: Effective prompts should provide relevant context to the language model. For example:

   - Context-free Prompt: *"Translate this sentence: 'Hello' to French."*

   - Context-rich Prompt: *"Translate this informal greeting: 'Hello' to French, taking into account that it is used in informal conversations among friends."*

3. **Precision**: Effective prompts should be formulated in a precise manner, guiding the model's behavior and output. For example:

- Vague Prompt: *"Generate a report."*

  Precise Prompt: *"Generate a monthly sales report for the first quarter of the year 2022, including total sales, sales by product category, and a trend analysis."*

- Unclear Prompt: *"Write a story about a dog."*

  Precise Prompt: *"Compose a heartwarming story about a loyal golden retriever named Buddy, who helps a young girl overcome her fear of the dark and teaches her valuable life lessons about courage and friendship."*

- Ambiguous Prompt: *"Describe a meal."*

  Precise Prompt: *"Describe a traditional Italian pasta dish, specifically spaghetti carbonara, highlighting its key ingredients, cooking method, and presentation, as well as its cultural significance and popular variations."*

4. **Sensitivity**: Effective prompts should be mindful of biases and ethical considerations. For example:

- Biased Prompt: *"Describe an ideal candidate for a software engineering job."*

- Ethical Prompt: *"Describe the qualifications, skills, and experience required for a software engineering job without including any gender, race, or age-related biases."*

5. **Creativity**: Use creativity to generate engaging prompts that stimulate the model's ability to generate diverse and creative responses. For example:

- Boring Prompt: *"Write a poem about flowers."*

- Creative Prompt: *"Compose a poetic ode to the ephemeral beauty of cherry blossoms in spring, capturing their delicate petals, sweet fragrance, and fleeting existence."*

By incorporating these examples of clear, context-rich, precise, ethical, and creative prompts, users can effectively leverage prompt engineering techniques to guide language models and generate accurate, coherent, and desired outputs in various applications and use cases.

 Ask the Expert

In this section, we are going to feed some prompts to ChatGPT AI Model and analyze how they stack up against the 5 key attributes of good prompt writing skills.

Prompt 1:

"Create a travel brochure for a cruise company targeting Gen Z for a 10-day trip to Japan."

Expert Analysis of Prompt 1:

1. Clarity: The prompt is clear in terms of the task to be performed, which is to create a travel brochure for a cruise company targeting Gen Z for a 10-day trip to Japan. It specifies the purpose and the target audience of the brochure.

2. Context: The prompt provides context in terms of the cruise company, the target audience (Gen Z), and the destination (Japan). This context helps guide the direction of the response and ensures that the generated content aligns with the intended purpose of the travel brochure.

3. Precision: The prompt is relatively precise in terms of the desired output, which is a travel brochure. However, it does not specify other details such as the theme, tone, or specific information to be included in the brochure, which may require further clarification for more precise guidance.

4. Sensitivity: The prompt does not raise any ethical or sensitive concerns, as it simply asks for a travel brochure for a cruise company targeting Gen Z for a trip to Japan without any sensitive or controversial topics involved.

5. Creativity: The prompt allows room for creativity, as it does not impose any strict limitations or constraints on the content, format, or style of the travel brochure. This allows the AI model to generate creative and engaging content that may appeal to the target audience.

Overall, prompt scores well in terms of clarity and context, but may benefit from additional precision and specificity for more effective guidance. It also allows for creativity and does not raise any sensitivity concerns.

Let us do an iteration to address the issue of precision and specificity in the commentary from the expert.

Revised Prompt 1:

"Create a travel brochure for a cruise company targeting Gen Z for a 10-day trip to Japan using less than 200 words. Use a friendly, engaging tone."

Analysis of Revised Prompt 1:

1. Clarity: The prompt is clear in terms of the task to be performed, which is to create a travel brochure for a cruise company targeting Gen Z for a 10-day trip to Japan. It also specifies the word limit for the brochure (less than 200 words) and the desired tone (friendly and engaging).

2. Context: The prompt provides context in terms of the cruise company, the target audience (Gen Z), the destination (Japan), and the desired tone (friendly and engaging). This context helps guide the direction of the response and ensures that the generated content aligns with the intended purpose and tone of the travel brochure.

3. Precision: The prompt is more precise compared to the previous prompt, as it specifies the word limit for the brochure (less than 200 words) and the desired tone (friendly and engaging). This provides more specific guidance to the AI model on the desired output.

4. Sensitivity: The prompt does not raise any ethical or sensitivity concerns, as it simply asks for a travel brochure for a cruise company targeting Gen Z for a trip to Japan, in a friendly and engaging tone.

5. Creativity: The prompt allows room for creativity, as it does not impose any strict limitations on the content, format, or style of the travel brochure, except for the desired tone. This allows the AI model to generate creative and engaging content within the given constraints.

Overall, the revised prompt scores well in terms of clarity, context, precision, and sensitivity. It also allows for creativity and provides specific guidance, making it an effective prompt for generating a travel brochure for a cruise company targeting Gen Z for a 10-day trip to Japan with a friendly and engaging tone in less than 200 words.

Prompt 2:

"Create a tip sheet on how to identify the red flags of a phishing attack for an employee security awareness training program. Keep it under 100 words. Write as a subject matter expert."

Analysis of Prompt 2:

1. Clarity: The prompt is clear in terms of the task to be performed, which is to create a tip sheet on how to identify the red flags of a phishing attack. It also specifies the purpose of the tip sheet, which is for an employee security awareness training program, and the desired length (under 100 words).

2. Context: The prompt provides context in terms of the purpose of the tip sheet, which is for an employee security awareness training program, and the topic, which is identifying red flags of a phishing attack. This context helps guide the direction of the response and ensures that the generated content is relevant and useful for the intended audience and purpose.

3. Precision: The prompt is precise in terms of the desired length of the tip sheet (under 100 words). This provides specific guidance to the AI model on the length of the response, which is an important aspect of prompt engineering for creating concise and effective content.

4. Sensitivity: The prompt does not raise any ethical or sensitivity concerns, as it simply asks for a tip sheet on identifying red flags of a phishing attack for an employee security awareness training program. However, it is important to ensure that the generated content is factually accurate and does not promote unethical or harmful behavior related to phishing attacks.

5. Creativity: The prompt allows room for creativity in terms of how the tip sheet is formatted and presented within the given length constraint. It also requires expertise in the subject matter of identifying red flags of a phishing attack, which allows the AI model to generate accurate and informative content.

Overall, this prompt scores well in terms of clarity, context, precision, and sensitivity. It also allows for creativity and requires subject matter expertise, making it an effective prompt for generating a tip sheet on identifying red flags of a phishing attack for an employee security awareness training program, keeping it under 100 words, and writing as a subject matter expert.

Prompt 3:

"Create a playful tagline for a soy-based health drink targeted at college students. Keep the tagline under 5 words."

Analysis of Prompt 3:

1. Clarity: The prompt is clear in terms of the task to be performed, which is to create a playful tagline for a soy-based health drink targeted at college students. It also specifies the desired length of the tagline (under 5 words), which provides clear guidance to the AI model.

2. Context: The prompt provides context in terms of the target audience (college students) and the product (soy-based health drink). This context helps guide the direction of the response and ensures that the generated tagline is relevant and appealing to the intended audience.

3. Precision: The prompt is precise in terms of the desired length of the tagline (under 5 words). This provides specific guidance to the AI model on the length constraint, which is an important aspect of prompt engineering for creating concise and impactful taglines.

4. Sensitivity: The prompt does not raise any ethical or sensitivity concerns, as it simply asks for a playful tagline for a soy-based health drink targeted at college students. However, it is important to ensure that the generated tagline does not promote any false claims or harmful behavior related to health or nutrition.

5. Creativity: The prompt allows room for creativity in terms of coming up with a playful and catchy tagline for the soy-based health drink. It requires the AI model to generate a concise and impactful tagline that resonates with the playful and energetic nature of college students.

Overall, the prompt scores well in terms of clarity, context, precision, and sensitivity. It also allows for creativity and requires the AI model to come up with a concise and engaging tagline for a soy-based health drink targeted at college students, keeping it under 5 words.

💡 Tips for Getting the Most Out of Prompt Responses

1. **Be Specific:** When crafting prompts, it's important to be clear and specific about what you want from the model. Avoid vague or generic instructions, and instead provide precise details and context. This helps the model better understand your intent and generate relevant and accurate responses.

2. **Experiment with Prompts:** Prompt engineering is an iterative process. Don't be afraid to experiment with different prompt styles, instructions, and parameter settings to fine-tune the model's output. Try different approaches and iterate based on the results to optimize the prompts for the desired output.

3. **Improve Accuracy with Step-By-Step Prompts:** While ChatGPT may not excel in math, users can utilize their prompt engineering

expertise to improve the generated results. For example, including phrases like "Let's do this step-by-step" in the prompt can significantly enhance ChatGPT's ability to solve word-based math problems.

Hands-on Lab Exercises

It is now time for you to do some lab exercises outlined below to test your understanding of the foundation principles of good prompt writing. I encourage you to solicit feedback on the prompts that you write so that you can improve them iteratively.

- **Clarity**:

  Question 1: Rewrite the following prompt to make it clearer: *"Write an essay on dogs."*

  Question 2: Which of the following prompts is the clearest for a creative writing task?

  a) *"Write a story about a boy and his pet."*

  b) *"Compose a narrative about a child and their animal companion."*

  c) *"Create a tale featuring a young protagonist and their loyal pet."*

- **Context**:

  Question 3: Create a prompt for a persuasive speech on the topic of environmental conservation for a high school audience.

  Question 4: How would you modify the following prompt to provide more context? *"Design a logo for a restaurant."*

- **Precision**:

  Question 5: Rewrite the following prompt to make it more precise: *"Describe a beautiful sunset."*

  Question 6: Which of the following prompts is the most precise for a research paper topic?

  a) *"Write about climate change."*

b) *"Examine the impact of climate change on polar ice caps."*

c) *"Discuss the causes, effects, and mitigation strategies of climate change on global ecosystems."*

- **Sensitivity:**

    <u>Question 7</u>: Create a prompt for a public speaking task on the topic of mental health awareness, taking into consideration potential sensitivity concerns.

    <u>Question 8</u>: How would you revise the following prompt to be more sensitive? *"Write an essay on the benefits of a meat-based diet."*

- **Creativity:**

    <u>Question 9</u>: Generate a creative writing prompt that encourages students to think imaginatively and come up with unique ideas.

    <u>Question 10</u>: How can you modify the following prompt to promote creativity? *"Design a poster for a safety campaign."*

Answer Key:

1. *Write an essay about the different breeds of dogs and their characteristics.*

2. *Compose a narrative about a child and their animal companion.*

3. *Deliver a persuasive speech on the importance of environmental conservation, focusing on specific actions individuals can take in their daily lives, for a high school audience.*

4. *Design a logo for a seafood restaurant with a nautical theme, featuring elements such as a lighthouse, anchor, and waves.*

5. *Describe a breathtaking sunset over the Pacific Ocean, capturing the vivid colors of the sky as the sun sets below the horizon.*

6. *Discuss the causes, effects, and mitigation strategies of climate change on global ecosystems.*

7. *Deliver a speech on mental health awareness, addressing the importance of destigmatizing mental illness, promoting self-care, and seeking professional help when needed, while respecting the privacy and confidentiality of individuals' mental health challenges.*

8. *Explore the advantages of different dietary choices, including meat-based diets, in an informative essay. Discuss the various perspectives and factors related to this topic, such as cultural preferences, nutritional considerations, and personal beliefs. Remember to present a balanced view, acknowledging both the benefits and potential drawbacks of different dietary approaches.*

9. *Write a short story from the perspective of an inanimate object, such as a pencil or a pair of shoes, experiencing an adventurous journey.*

10. *Design a poster for a safety campaign that creatively communicates the importance of wearing helmets while riding bicycles, using visually engaging graphics and catchy slogans to encourage safe biking habits.*

The key attributes of good prompt writing are:

- Clarity: Effective prompts should be unambiguous, providing precise instructions to the language model.
- Context: Effective prompts should provide relevant context to the language model.
- Precision: Effective prompts should be formulated in a precise manner, guiding the model's behavior and output.
- Sensitivity: Effective prompts should be mindful of biases and ethical considerations.
- Creativity: Effective prompts should use creativity to generate engaging prompts that stimulate the model's ability to generate diverse and creative responses.
- Experimenting with Prompts: Prompt Engineering is an iterative process.

CHAPTER 4

Advanced Topics in Prompt Engineering

In this Chapter the topics covered include

- Multi-Turn Engineering
- Contextual Information
- System Messages
- Prompt Engineering with Constraints
- Template Based Forms
- Data Augmentation
- Step-by-Step Prompts
- Prompt Engineering with Rewards Models

Deep Dive Into Advanced Topics

1. **Multi-Turn Conversations**: Multi-turn conversations involve creating prompts as dynamic and interactive conversations with the language model. This allows for a back-and-forth exchange of information, simulating a conversation with the model. This can be useful for tasks that require context from previous turns to generate accurate responses. For example:

   Prompt:

   User: *"Book me a flight from New York to London."*

   Assistant: *"Sure, when would you like to depart and return?"*

   User: *"I want to leave on May 1st and return on May 5th."*

Assistant: *"Great! Let me find the available flights for you."*

In this example, the prompt includes multiple turns of conversation between the user and the assistant, providing context for the flight booking task.

2. **Contextual Information**: Including relevant contextual information in the prompt can guide the model's understanding and generate more accurate responses. Context can be provided explicitly in the prompt or extracted from previous turns in a multi-turn conversation.

    Prompt: *"Translate the following English text to French: {text}"*

    Including the source and target languages in the prompt provides contextual information for the translation task.

3. **System Messages**: Using system messages at the beginning of the prompt can help set the context and behavior of the language model. System messages are used to provide instructions or guidance to the model, and the model may interpret and respond accordingly.

    Prompt: *"System: You are a weather assistant."*

    User: *"What's the weather like in Paris today?"*

    The system message sets the role and behavior of the model as a weather assistant, guiding its response to the user's query.

4. **Prompt Engineering with Constraints**: Including constraints in the prompt can ensure that the model's output adheres to specific requirements or limitations. Constraints can be in the form of explicit instructions or limitations on the generated output.

    Prompt: *"Write a story about a cat {length: short} {genre: fantasy}."*

    Including constraints such as story length (short) and genre (fantasy) in the prompt guides the model in generating a story that meets those specific criteria.

5. **Template-Based Forms**: Using template-based forms involves structuring the prompt as a form with predefined fields and values. This can be useful for tasks that require structured responses or filling out forms.

   Prompt: *"Please fill out the following form: Name: {name}, Age: {age}, Gender: {gender}"*

   The prompt is structured as a form with fields for name, age, and gender, and the model generates responses by filling in the corresponding values.

   Prompt: *"Write an NDA for an employee using the template: Employee Name: [e.g., Tim Leno] Company Name: [e.g., XYZ Company Inc.] Company Industry: [Banking/Healthcare/Pharma/Technology] Event: [signing/termination/separation] Duration: [6 months, etc.]"*

   This prompt generates a Non-Disclosure Agreement

6. **Data Augmentation**: Data augmentation is a technique used in data science and machine learning to artificially increase the size of a dataset by creating new data samples from the original data. It involves applying various modifications or transformations to the original data to create new examples that are slightly different but still representative of the underlying concept or pattern.

   Here are three examples of data augmentation:

   - *Image Data Augmentation:* In image data augmentation, transformations such as rotation, flipping, cropping, and adding noise can be applied to images. This can help to improve the accuracy of image classification models. For example, a model that is trained on a dataset of augmented images will be more likely to correctly classify images that are rotated or flipped than a model that is trained on a dataset of non-augmented images.

   - *Text Data Augmentation:* In text data augmentation, transformations such as synonym replacement, word order shuffling, and noise addition can be applied to text. This can help to improve the accuracy of text classification models. For example, a model that is trained on a dataset of augmented text will be more likely to correctly classify text that is written in a different style than the text on which it was trained.

- *Financial Data Augmentation:* Financial data augmentation is a technique used to expand and enhance existing financial datasets. By generating additional data points and scenarios, it provides a broader perspective and helps uncover insights about financial risk, portfolio performance, and market conditions.

Example Prompt: "Given the historical financial data of Company X, augment the dataset to simulate potential scenarios of financial risk. Generate additional data points reflecting changes in key financial metrics such as revenue, expenses, and profitability. Consider both optimistic and pessimistic scenarios for the next quarter and provide insights on the potential impact on the company's financial risk profile."

Source Data: Historical financial data (e.g., balance sheets, income statements) of various companies

Augmentation: The generated data points will simulate different financial scenarios for Company X, enabling risk analysts to assess the potential risks associated with various financial outcomes. This augmented dataset can help in evaluating the company's resilience to changing market conditions and making informed decisions regarding risk management strategies.

Example Prompt: Generate a new financial plan for Company Y that is similar to this one, but with a different set of goals.

(In this case, the Company's board of directors may want to increase the company's profits by 10% in the next year, the finance manager would use the data augmentation prompt to generate a new financial forecast that is consistent with this goal. The new financial forecast would then be used to help the company develop a plan to achieve this goal.)

Source data: A financial plan that has been created using a variety of data sources and goals.

Augmentation: The prompt will generate a new financial plan that is similar to the source data, but with a different set of goals. This can be useful for exploring different financial planning options.

Data augmentation is used to overcome the limitations of having limited data and can help improve the accuracy and robustness of machine learning models.

7. **Step-by-Step:** Step-by-step prompts are designed to guide a language model like ChatGPT to generate responses in a structured and organized manner, following a sequence of steps or instructions. These prompts provide a clear framework for the model to follow, resulting in more coherent and relevant outputs. Step-by-step prompts also help in improving the accuracy of Large Language Models like ChatGPT due to their current limitations in reasoning capabilities.

   Example 1: Recipe Generation

   Prompt: *"Generate a recipe for a delicious chocolate cake. Use a step-by-step approach and include detailed instructions."*

   In this example, the prompt explicitly mentions the use of a step-by-step approach and requests for detailed instructions. The model can then generate a recipe for a chocolate cake, following a logical sequence of steps, such as mixing ingredients, preparing the batter, baking, and frosting the cake. The resulting output is likely to be well-organized and easy to follow.

   Example 2: DIY Project Instructions

   Prompt: *"Write a set of instructions for building a birdhouse. Use a step-by-step approach and include clear guidance."*

   In this scenario, the prompt directs the model to adopt a step-by-step approach and provides clear guidance for building a birdhouse. The model can then generate instructions that outline each step of the construction process, including cutting wood, assembling pieces, drilling holes, and painting. The generated output is expected to be organized and coherent, providing a clear set of instructions for the DIY project.

8. **Prompt Engineering with Reward Models**: Incorporating reward models involves using additional information or feedback to guide the model's output. This can be done by providing rewards or scoring the generated output based on predefined criteria and using reinforcement learning techniques to optimize the model's responses.

   Example: Prompt: *"Generate a creative and engaging product description. You will be rewarded based on the length, uniqueness, and use of persuasive language in your description."*

   The prompt provides specific criteria for the product description and offers rewards based on those criteria, encouraging the model to generate a high-quality description.

These are some advanced topics in prompt engineering that can be utilized to optimize the performance of language models for various tasks and applications. Experimenting and iterating with different prompt engineering techniques can help fine-tune the model's outputs to meet specific requirements and achieve desired results.

Template-Based Forms

Template-based forms are a crucial aspect of prompt engineering that can greatly benefit professionals who want to leverage the power of ChatGPT in their business. These forms provide a structured and organized way to generate prompts, making it easier to elicit specific and desired responses from the language model. Let us take a deep dive with some examples:

1. **Code Generation Prompt**: *"Write a Python function that calculates the sum of two numbers. The function should take two arguments, {arg1} and {arg2}, and return the sum as the output."*

In this example, the prompt includes constraints on the required function to be generated, specifying the input arguments (arg1, arg2) and the desired output (sum of two numbers).

2. **Meal Plan Template Prompt:** Here's an example of using a template to create a meal plan for a week, incorporating variables like type of meal, restrictions, budget, meal-type, etc.

    "Write a function that generates a meal plan for a week. The function should take four arguments: {meal_type}, {dietary_restrictions}, {budget}, and {meal_categories}. The output should be a structured meal plan that fits within these constraints."

3. **Image Captioning Prompt**: *"Generate a caption for the following image: {image}. The caption should not exceed {max_length} words and should describe the image accurately."*

    In this example, the prompt includes a constraint on the maximum length of the generated caption and provides guidance on the desired content, i.e., accurately describing the given image.

4. **Content Generation with Specific Keywords Prompt**: *"Write a blog post about {topic} that includes the keywords: {keyword1}, {keyword2}, and {keyword3}. The blog post should be {length} words long and provide valuable information about the topic."*

    In this example, the prompt includes constraints on the topic, keywords, length, and content of the blog post, thus guiding the model to generate a post that includes the specified keywords and meets the desired length and content requirements.

5. **Conversation Response with Specific Tone Prompt**: *"You are an AI chatbot that responds to customer queries. Respond to the following user query in a polite and friendly tone: '{query}'"*

    In this example, the prompt sets the context and behavior of the chatbot as a polite and friendly assistant, providing a constraint on the desired tone of the generated response to the user query.

6. **Story Writing with Given Plot Points Prompt**: *"Write a short story with the following plot points: {plot1}, {plot2}, and {plot3}. The story should have a clear beginning, middle, and end, and should be at least {min_length} words long."*

   In this example, the prompt includes constraints on the plot points to be incorporated into the story, the desired structure (beginning, middle, and end), and the minimum length of the story.

7. **Resume Generation Template:**

   Template: *"Name: {name}\nContact Information: {contact_info}\nEducation: {education}\nExperience: {experience}\nSkills: {skills}"*

   Prompt: *"Please generate a resume for the following person:\nName: John Doe\nContact Information: john.doe@email.com, (123) 456-7890\nEducation: Bachelor's in Computer Science\nExperience: 5 years as a Software Engineer\nSkills: Java, Python, C++"*

   In this example, the template is provided as the structure for a resume. The prompt includes the specific details for the person John Doe, which can be filled in the template to generate a personalized resume.

Including constraints in prompts can help guide the model's output and ensure that it meets specific requirements, making prompt engineering a powerful technique for customizing the model's responses according to the desired criteria or limitations.

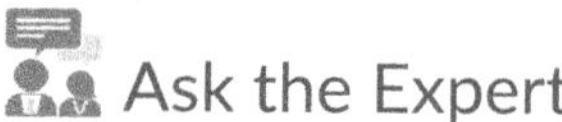

Ask the Expert

Exercise 1: Event Invitation Template:

Prompt: *"Please generate an invitation for the following event:\nEvent Name: Annual Company Picnic\nEvent Date: 05/20/2023\nEvent Time: 12:00 PM - 4:00 PM\nEvent Location: Central Park, New York City\nEvent Details: Food, games, and team-building activities for all employees and their families"*

> **Generated Invitation:**
>
> "You're Invited! Join us for the Annual Company Picnic on 05/20/2023 from 12:00 PM - 4:00 PM at Central Park, New York City. RSVP to confirm your attendance. Food, games, and team-building activities for all employees and their families will be available."

📝 Expert Analysis of Template

Let us analyze this template based on the key attributes of a good prompt:

- Contextual Programming: The generated invitation incorporates the details provided in the prompt, including the event name, date, time, location, and event details. The language model has effectively used the provided information to create a relevant and contextually accurate invitation.

- Clarity & Language Tone: The generated invitation is clear and concise, conveying the event details in a straightforward manner. The tone is inviting and friendly, creating a positive impression for potential attendees.

- Length & Conciseness: The generated invitation is concise and not overly long, providing the necessary information without unnecessary elaboration. It avoids redundant or repetitive information, keeping the invitation focused.

- Iterative Refinement: Based on feedback and performance analysis, the template can be refined iteratively to enhance the generated prompt. This may include adjusting the tone, style, or length based on the desired communication goals or audience preferences.

Overall, this example illustrates how template-based forms can be used to generate clear, concise, and contextually accurate prompts for specific business use cases, such as creating invitations for events, and highlights the importance of contextual programming, clarity, language tone, length, and iterative refinement in prompt engineering for effective communication with users.

<u>*Exercise 2*</u>: **Prompt Engineering with Constraints for a Travel Agency Chatbot:**

Prompt:

"You are a chatbot for a travel agency helping a user plan their vacation. The user wants to visit a destination within a budget of $1000. Generate a response that suggests travel destinations within the given budget."

Chatbot: "Great! Based on your budget of $1000, here are some travel destinations you can consider:

1. Mexico City, Mexico - With its rich history, vibrant culture, and delicious cuisine, Mexico City offers a diverse range of attractions and experiences within a budget-friendly price range. You can explore ancient ruins, visit museums, indulge in local street food, and enjoy the city's nightlife.

2. Bali, Indonesia - Known for its beautiful beaches, lush landscapes, and affordable accommodations, Bali is a popular travel destination for budget-conscious travelers. You can enjoy surfing, hiking, yoga, and cultural experiences, while also relishing delicious local cuisine and exploring the island's temples.

3. Budapest, Hungary - This picturesque European city offers a rich blend of history, architecture, and cultural experiences at an affordable cost. You can soak in the thermal baths, visit historic sites like Buda Castle and Fisherman's Bastion, and indulge in local Hungarian cuisine.

4. Lisbon, Portugal - With its charming streets, historic landmarks, and coastal vibe, Lisbon is an affordable destination for travelers seeking a mix of culture and relaxation. You can explore the city's narrow alleys, visit iconic sites like Belem Tower and Jeronimos Monastery, and enjoy authentic Portuguese food.

5. Hanoi, Vietnam - This bustling city in Southeast Asia offers a unique blend of cultural heritage, street food, and affordability. You can explore the Old Quarter, visit historical sites like Hoàn Kiem Lake and the Temple of Literature, and savor delicious Vietnamese cuisine.

📝 Expert Analysis of Template:

- Contextual Programming: The generated response addresses the user's request for travel destinations within a budget of $1000, providing relevant suggestions that fit the given criteria.

- Clarity & Language Tone: The response provides clear and concise information about each destination, highlighting their attractions, cultural experiences, and affordability, in a friendly and informative tone.

- Length & Conciseness: The response provides succinct suggestions without unnecessary elaboration, ensuring the information is concise and easy to understand.

- Iterative Refinement: The template can be refined iteratively based on user feedback and performance analysis, incorporating additional destinations, or updating information to align with user preferences or changing travel trends.

Overall, this example showcases how prompt engineering can be used to generate relevant and informative responses for a travel agency chatbot, considering contextual programming, clarity, language tone, length, and iterative refinement to provide value to users.

Exercise 3: Chatbot for Food Delivery

Prompt: "You are a chatbot for a food delivery service. The user wants to place an order. Generate a response that prompts the user to provide their name, contact number, and order details. Include a welcome message and walk thru a simulated conversation with a customer John Doe."

Prompt:

> *You are a chatbot for a food delivery service. John Doe wants to place an order. Generate a response that prompts the user to provide their name, contact number, and order details. Include a welcome message and walk us through the conversation.*

Chatbot: "Hello, and welcome to our food delivery service! We are excited to assist you with placing an order. To get started, could you please provide us with your name?"

John Doe: "Sure! My name is John Doe."

Chatbot: "Thank you, John! Next, could you please provide us with your contact number? This will help us ensure a smooth delivery process."

John Doe: "Sure! My contact number is +1 (123) 456-7890."

Chatbot: "Great! Finally, could you please provide us with the details of your order? You can include the items you would like to order, any specific dietary preferences, and any special instructions."

John Doe: "Sure! I would like to order a large pepperoni pizza with extra cheese and a side of garlic bread."

Chatbot: "Thank you for providing the order details, John! We will process your order and ensure it is delivered to you as per your preferences. Is there anything else you would like to add or modify in your order?"

John Doe: "No, that's it. Thank you!"

Chatbot: "You're welcome, John! We will confirm your order and provide you with an estimated delivery time. If you have any further questions or need assistance, feel free to ask. Enjoy your meal!"

 Expert Analysis of Template:

- In the above conversation, the chatbot starts with a welcome message to greet the user (John Doe) and then prompts for the user's name, contact number, and order details.

- The prompts are clear, concise, friendly, and efficient in guiding the user through the process of placing an order.

- The chatbot collects all the necessary information, confirms the order, and provides additional assistance if needed.

Prompt engineering plays a crucial role in creating prompts that are tailored to the context of the conversation, ensuring a smooth and personalized experience for the user.

 Tips for Getting the Most Out of Prompt Responses

1. **Design Conversations with Clear System Messages**: When using multi-turn conversations, it is crucial to include clear and explicit system messages to guide the model's behavior. System messages can set the context, tone, and role of the AI assistant in the conversation. For example:

   System Message: "You are an AI assistant helping a customer book a flight ticket."

   This helps establish the desired role and behavior of the AI assistant in the conversation, leading to more coherent and relevant responses.

2. **Use Templates for Structured Prompts**: Template-based prompts can be powerful for guiding the model's responses in the desired direction. You can create templates with placeholders for specific information you want the model to generate. For example:

   "Book a flight from [departure city] to [destination city] on [date] for [number of passengers] passengers."

By using templates, you can provide structure and constraints to the model's responses, ensuring they align with the desired format or information.

3. **Use Step-by-Step Prompts** Step-by-Step prompts provide a structure and framework for the language model to generate outputs that follow a logical sequence of instructions, resulting in accurate, coherent, and relevant responses. For example:

   "Generate a step-by-step guide on how to graph a linear function. Include all the necessary steps and details for plotting the graph."

Hands-on Lab Exercises

It is now time to test your skills on the above topics and showcase your mastery in advanced prompt engineering topics.

1) **Template-Based Forms**:

   a. *Exercise*: Create a template-based form prompt for collecting user information to register for an online course. The form should include fields for name, email, phone number, and preferred course category. Use placeholders for user input and indicate the expected format for each field.

   b. *Exercise*: Create a template-based form prompt for collecting feedback from users about a recently launched product. The form should include fields for product name, feedback type (positive/negative/neutral), and comments. Use appropriate placeholders for user input and specify the maximum word limit for comments.

   c. *Exercise*: Create a template-based form prompt for collecting feedback from users about a recent event. The form should include fields for event name, feedback rating (1-5), and suggestions for improvement. Use placeholders for user input and specify the format for the feedback rating field.

d. *Exercise:* Create a template-based form prompt for collecting user feedback on a mobile app. The form should include fields for app name, feedback rating (1-10), and suggestions for improvement. Use placeholders for user input and indicate the required format for the feedback rating field.

e. *Exercise:* Write a toast for a celebration with the following details: Type of Event: [wedding/birthday/marriage anniversary/graduation] Recipient: [bride/groom/birthday person/graduate] Relationship: [friend/sibling/parent/grandparent/mother-in-law] Details to Include: [a special memory/their personality/their hobbies/funny inside joke] Tone: [funny/sentimental/inspiring].

f. *Exercise:* Create a residential lease agreement for a property with the following details: Property Type: [apartment/house/condominium] Property Address: [insert property address] State [Insert State] Rent Amount: [$1,000 month/$2,000 month] Lease Term: [3 months/6 months/12 months].

2) **Multi-Turn Conversations:**

a. *Exercise:* Design a multi-turn conversation prompt for a chatbot that assists users in booking a flight ticket. The conversation should start with the user asking for flight options, followed by the chatbot providing flight details, and finally, the user confirming the booking with payment information. Include appropriate user and chatbot responses in the conversation.

b. *Exercise:* Design a multi-turn conversation prompt for a customer support chatbot. The conversation should start with the user reporting a technical issue, followed by the chatbot asking for additional details, and then providing troubleshooting steps. Finally, the user confirms if the issue is resolved or requires further assistance.

c. _Exercise:_ Design a multi-turn conversation prompt for a virtual personal assistant. The conversation should start with the user asking for a weather forecast, followed by the chatbot providing current weather details and suggesting activities based on the weather. The user then confirms the suggested activity or asks for an alternative suggestion.

3) **Prompt Engineering with Constraints:**

   a. _Exercise:_ Develop a prompt that generates a recipe recommendation for a user with specific dietary constraints. The constraints include being gluten-free, dairy-free, and low-carb. The prompt should ask for the user's preferred cuisine and meal type, and then generate a recipe suggestion that meets the dietary constraints.

   b. _Exercise:_ Develop a prompt that generates a movie recommendation for a user based on their preferred genre and release year. The prompt should also include a constraint that the movie should have a minimum rating of 8.0 on IMDb. Ask the user for their preferred genre and release year, and then generate a movie suggestion that meets the constraint.

   c. _Exercise:_ Develop a prompt that generates a book recommendation for a user with a constraint on the book's genre and length. The user prefers mystery novels and requires the book to be less than 300 pages. The prompt should ask for the user's preferred genre and length, and then generate a book suggestion that meets the constraint.

4) **Step-by-Step Prompt:**

   a. _Exercise:_ Write a prompt to create a step-by-step guide to calculate the area of a circle.

   b. _Exercise:_ Write a prompt to create a step-by-step guide for baking chocolate cookies for your son's birthday event.

In this chapter, we have covered advanced topics in prompt engineering, including:

- Multi-Turn Conversations: Creating prompts as dynamic conversations to simulate back-and-forth exchanges with the model.

- Contextual Information: Including relevant contextual information in prompts to guide the model's understanding and generate accurate responses.

- System Messages: Using system messages to set the context and behavior of the model.

- Prompt Engineering with Constraints: Including constraints in prompts to guide the model's output and ensure adherence to specific requirements.

- Template-Based Forms: Structuring prompts as forms with predefined fields and values for structured responses.

- Data Augmentation: Using data augmentation techniques to artificially increase the size of a dataset and improve model accuracy.

- Step-By-Step Prompts: Step-by-step prompts are designed to guide a language model like ChatGPT to generate responses in a structured and organized manner, following a sequence of steps or instructions.

- Prompt Engineering with Reward Models: Incorporating reward models to guide the model's output based on predefined criteria and using reinforcement learning techniques.

These advanced topics can be used to optimize the performance of language models for various tasks and applications by fine-tuning the model's outputs to meet specific requirements and achieve desired results.

CHAPTER 5

Best Practices in Prompt Engineering

In this chapter, the topics covered include:

- Understanding the Nuances of Language and Tone
- Testing and Iterating Prompts for Improved Performance
- Incorporating Feedback from AI Models to Refine Prompts

✒ Understanding the Nuances of Language and Tone

Language and tone play a crucial role in prompt engineering as they determine how the model interprets and responds to prompts. Here are 5 specific examples of best practices along with expert comments, to understand the nuances of language and tone in prompt engineering:

1. **Clarity of Instruction**: Be clear and specific in your instructions to the model. Use simple and concise language to convey your intent effectively. Avoid ambiguity or vague phrases that may result in misinterpretation. For example:

   Prompt: *"Translate this English sentence into French: 'The weather is fine.'"*

   Expert Comment: Using clear and simple language in the prompt helps the model understand the task accurately and generate an appropriate response.

2. **Tone and Style**: Determine the desired tone and style of the output. Use language that matches the tone and style you want the model to emulate. For example:

   Prompt: *"Write a persuasive email to convince customers to try our new product."*

   Expert Comment: Using words like "persuasive" and "convince" sets the tone for the model to generate a persuasive email that aligns with the desired style of communication.

3. **Context Awareness**: Provide relevant context to guide the model's understanding of the prompt. Include relevant information, keywords, or specific details that can help the model generate appropriate responses. For example:

   Prompt: *"As a customer service representative, respond to this customer complaint about a delayed delivery."*

   Expert Comment: Including the role of the customer service representative and the context of a delayed delivery helps the model understand the scenario and generate a response that addresses the customer's concern.

4. **Avoiding Bias and Controversial Content**: Be mindful of bias and controversial content in prompts. Avoid using language that may lead to biased or offensive responses from the model. For example:

   Prompt: *"Write a review of this political candidate, highlighting their positive qualities."*

   Expert Comment: Avoiding biased language and ensuring a balanced approach in the prompt can help the model generate a fair and unbiased review of the political candidate.

5. **Localization and Cultural Sensitivity**: Consider the cultural context and language nuances of the target audience. Use appropriate language, idioms, and references that are relevant to the audience's culture and region. For example:

Prompt: *"Write a marketing campaign for a product targeted towards a Japanese audience."*

Expert Comment: Ensuring the use of appropriate language, cultural references, and marketing strategies relevant to the Japanese audience can help the model generate a more effective marketing campaign.

6. **Language and Tone:** They play a crucial role in prompt engineering as they determine how the model interprets and responds to prompts. Let us now look at a bad example:

    Bad Example: *"Write an email to convince customers to buy our product, but don't use any marketing jargon."*

    Expert Comment: This prompt contains contradictory instructions, asking the model to convince customers without using marketing jargon, which may confuse the model and result in an ineffective response.

Understanding the nuances of language and tone in prompt engineering is crucial for obtaining desired outputs from language models like ChatGPT. Following the above best practices can help you craft effective prompts that result in accurate and contextually relevant responses from the model.

Testing and Iterating Prompts for Improved Performance

Testing and iterating are critical steps in prompt engineering to ensure improved performance of language models like ChatGPT. Let us explore specific examples along with expert comments to understand the best practices for testing and iterating prompts:

1. **A/B Testing:** Conduct A/B testing by using multiple prompts and comparing the outputs to determine which one performs better. For example:

Prompt A: *"Write a product description for a smartphone focusing on its features."*

Prompt B: *"Compose a marketing copy for a mobile device highlighting its specifications."*

Expert Comment: A/B testing can help you identify which prompt generates a more accurate and desired output, allowing you to fine-tune your prompts for better performance.

2. **Prompt Variations**: Experiment with different prompt variations to understand the model's response to different inputs. For example:

   Prompt 1: *"Write a blog post about the benefits of exercising."*

   Prompt 2: *"Compose an article discussing the advantages of regular physical activity."*

   Expert Comment: Testing prompt variations can help you identify which wording, structure, or tone resonates better with the model and yields more suitable outputs.

3. **Contextual Testing**: Test prompts in different contexts and scenarios to evaluate the model's ability to understand and respond. For example:

   Prompt 1: *"Write a news article about a political event that happened last year."*

   Prompt 2: *"Compose a report on a recent political development in the last 6 months."*

   Expert Comment: Contextual testing can help you assess the model's capability to understand and adapt to different timeframes, events, or scenarios, ensuring accurate and relevant responses.

4. **Input Length Testing**: Test prompts with varying input lengths to observe the model's response to different prompt lengths. For example:

   Prompt 1: *"Write a tweet about a new movie release in 10 words or less."*

Prompt 2: *"Compose a social media post discussing a recent film in 100 words or more."*

Expert Comment: Testing prompts with different input lengths can help you understand how the model performs with varying levels of information. Adjust prompts accordingly for optimal performance.

5. **Edge Case Testing**: Test prompts with unique or challenging scenarios to evaluate the model's ability to handle edge cases. For example:

    Prompt: *"Write a poem about modern technology in Shakespearean style."*

    Expert Comment: Edge case testing can help you assess the model's adaptability and creativity in generating responses for unconventional or unique prompts.

6. **Sentiment Testing**: Test prompts with varying sentiment tones, such as positive, negative, and neutral, to observe the model's ability to generate responses based on different sentiment cues. For example:

    Prompt 1: *"Write a social media post expressing excitement about the opening of a new restaurant."*

    Prompt 2: *"Compose a customer complaint email about a faulty product."*

    Sentiment testing can help you understand how the model interprets and responds to different sentiment tones. Refine prompts accordingly to achieve the desired sentiment in the generated outputs.

Testing and iterating prompts are crucial in prompt engineering to fine-tune and optimize the performance of language models. Experimenting with different prompts, variations, contexts, lengths, and edge cases can help you identify the best approach for obtaining desired outputs from ChatGPT, and can continuously improve the performance of your prompt engineering efforts.

Incorporating Feedback from AI Models to Refine Prompts

This is a major step in prompt engineering as it allows you to continuously improve and optimize your prompts based on the feedback received from the AI model. Here are some specific examples along with expert comments:

1. **Analyzing Model Output**: Review the generated outputs from the AI model and analyze them to identify patterns, trends, and areas for improvement. For example, you may notice that the model tends to produce responses that are too verbose or lack clarity in certain situations.

   Expert Comment: Analyzing the model's output can help you identify any recurring issues or limitations in the responses generated by the model, and provide insights on how to refine prompts to address these issues.

2. **Soliciting User Feedback**: Collect feedback from users who interact with the AI system and observe how they interact with the prompts. Ask for their opinions, suggestions, and insights on the quality, relevance, and effectiveness of the model's responses.

   Expert Comment: User feedback can provide valuable insights into the strengths and weaknesses of the model's responses from a user's perspective, and help you refine prompts to better align with user expectations and requirements.

3. **A/B Testing**: Conduct A/B testing by using different prompts or variations of prompts and compare the performance and effectiveness of the AI model to different prompts in generating desired outputs.

   Expert Comment: A/B testing can help you identify which prompts or variations of prompts are more effective in generating desired responses from the AI model. Refine prompts accordingly to optimize performance.

4. **Iterative Refinement**: Continuously iterate and refine prompts based on the feedback received from the AI model, users, and testing. Monitor the performance of the prompts over time to identify areas for further improvement.

   Expert Comment: Prompt refinement is an ongoing process. Iterative refinement based on feedback from various sources can help you continuously optimize and improve the effectiveness of your prompts in guiding the AI model to generate the desired responses.

Incorporating feedback from AI models is a crucial step in prompt engineering. It helps you to fine-tune prompts and align them with the evolving requirements and expectations of the AI system's outputs.

By carefully analyzing model outputs, soliciting user feedback, conducting A/B testing, and continuously refining prompts, you can improve the performance and effectiveness of your prompts in guiding the AI model to generate desired responses.

⚇⚇⚇ Enhancing Reliability of Responses

Generative AI Models are notorious for occasionally making up responses. Outlined below are some practical tips for enhancing reliability of the responses:

1. **Provide Explicit Guidance:** Clearly instruct the model to only provide information from reliable and credible sources. You can include prompts like, *"Please base your response on verifiable and reputable sources"* or *"Ensure that the information provided is accurate and supported by reliable data."*

2. **Specify Trusted Sources:** Guide the model by specifying the sources it should consider or refer to when generating factual information. For example, you can prompt the model with, *"Please use information from reputable publications like Forbes or The New York Times."*

3. **Encourage Citation or Attribution:** Prompt the model to cite its sources when providing specific facts or information. You can include instructions like, *"If you mention a statistic, please include the source so that it can be verified."*

4. **Implement Fact-Checking Mechanisms:** Integrate fact-checking tools or processes into the conversation flow. You can set up an additional step where the generated information is cross-checked against reliable sources or manually reviewed by a human to ensure accuracy.

5. **Request Multiple Perspectives:** Ask the model to consider various viewpoints or sources before providing a response. By prompting the model to consider different perspectives, it can help reduce bias and provide a more well-rounded answer.

 Give More "Think Time" to the Model.

When the model has more time to process and analyze the given prompt, it can explore a wider range of possibilities and generate more coherent and informed responses. Outlined below are some practical tips:

1. **Extend the Wait Time:** Allow the model more time to process and generate responses by increasing the time interval between the user's prompt and the model's response. This can be done by implementing delays or pauses in the conversation flow.

2. **Utilize System Messages:** Insert system messages in the conversation to indicate that the model can take its time to generate a thoughtful response. For example, you can include messages like *"Please take a moment to consider the best approach"* or *"We appreciate your patience while the model generates a detailed response."*

3. **Use Explicit Instructions:** Provide explicit instructions to the model, asking it to think deeply, consider different perspectives, or provide detailed explanations. For instance, you can prompt the

model with, *"Please take your time to analyze the data and provide a thorough analysis."*

4. **Experiment with Temperature:** Adjust the temperature parameter to influence the randomness and creativity of the model's responses. Higher values (e.g., 0.8) can introduce more randomness and exploration, while lower values (e.g., 0.2) can encourage more focused and deterministic responses.

Staying Up to Date with the Latest Advancements in Prompt Engineering

Staying up to date with the latest advancements in prompt engineering is essential to ensure that you are leveraging the most effective techniques and strategies to optimize the performance of your AI models. Here are some ways to stay updated:

1. **Follow Research Publications:** Keep an eye on research publications, journals, and conferences related to artificial intelligence, natural language processing, and prompt engineering. Stay updated with the latest research findings, techniques, and best practices shared by academic and research communities.

2. **Participate in Communities and Forums:** Join online communities, forums, and discussion groups related to prompt engineering, AI, and NLP. Engage in discussions, share ideas, and learn from fellow professionals and experts in the field.

3. **Attend Workshops and Conferences:** Attend workshops, conferences, and webinars related to prompt engineering, AI, and NLP. These events provide opportunities to learn from industry experts, engage in hands-on learning, and stay updated with the latest advancements in the field.

4. **Follow Industry Leaders and Influencers:** Follow thought leaders, influencers, and experts in the field of prompt engineering, AI, and NLP on social media platforms, blogs, and websites. Stay

updated with their latest insights, opinions, and recommendations on prompt engineering best practices.

💡 Tips for Getting the Most Out of Prompt Responses

1. **Be Specific**. Leave as little to interpretation as possible. Restrict the operational space by defining guardrails.

    Example: Instead of asking *"write a story,"* provide specific guidelines and restrictions, such as *"Write a short story about a detective solving a crime, in less than 500 words."*

2. **Be Descriptive**. Use analogies.

    Example: Instead of asking *"generate a product name,"* provide descriptive analogies, such as *"Generate a product name that sounds sleek and sophisticated, like a luxury car brand."*

3. **Double Down**. Sometimes you may need to repeat yourself to the model. Give instructions before and after your primary content, use an instruction and a cue, etc.

    Example: Instead of asking *"write a summary of this article,"* provide an instruction and a cue, such as *"Summarize the following article in one paragraph. Begin your summary with the main idea and include at least two supporting points."*

4. **Order Matters**. The order in which you present information to the model may impact the output. Whether you put instructions before your content (*"summarize the following…"*) or after (*"summarize the above…"*) can make a difference in output. Even the order of few-shot examples can matter. This is referred to as recency bias.

    Example: Instead of providing few-shot examples in a random order, present them in a logical order, such as from easiest to hardest or from general to specific.

5. **Give the model an "Out."** It can sometimes be helpful to give the model an alternative path if it is unable to complete the assigned task. For example, when asking a question over a piece of text,

you might include something like, *"Respond with 'not found' if the answer is not present"*. This can help the model avoid generating false responses.

Example: Instead of asking *"provide a synonym for the word 'big'"*, provide an alternative prompt such as *"if you can't think of a synonym for 'big,' provide an antonym instead."*

Hands-on Lab Exercises

Exercise 1: You are a seasoned traveler who loves to visit novel places. But you are very selective of the kind of hotels you would like to stay in for the trip duration. You are heading to Miami for a three-day trip. You usually book your trips on Expedia. Here is the exercise:

Pick the hotel of your choice in Miami. Select a sampling of the customer reviews on Expedia for this hotel. Select a larger data set of customer reviews (at least 10 or more for this exercise). Write a prompt to instruct ChatGPT to do the following:

(i)   Do a sentiment analysis on the customer reviews by doing a cut & paste of the customer review data.

(ii) Ask the model to summarize insights from the customer data.

(iii) Ask the model to compute the Net Promoter Score (NPS).

Lab Exercise 2: A/B Testing Prompt Variations

Objective: To perform A/B testing to compare the performance of different prompt variations in a language model.

Instructions:

1. Select a language model, such as GPT-3 or similar, and set up a controlled experiment environment.

2. Develop two or more prompt variations, using different prompt engineering techniques, such as template-based prompts, instruction-based prompts, or system/user messages.

3. Randomly assign participants to different prompt variations.

4. Provide the same input prompt to each group, but with variations of prompts.

5. Collect and analyze the output responses generated by the model for each group.

6. Compare and evaluate the performance of the prompt variations based on predefined metrics, such as relevance, coherence, creativity, or any other relevant criteria.

7. Draw conclusions and insights from A/B testing results and discuss the implications for prompt engineering strategies.

◎ Chapter Summary

In this chapter, we have covered some of the best practices in Prompt Engineering:

1. **Clarity of Instruction:**
   - Be clear and specific with your instructions.
   - Use simple and concise language.
   - Avoid ambiguity and vague phrases.
   - Provide relevant context to guide the model's understanding.

2. **Tone and Style:**
   - Consider the desired tone and style of the output.
   - Use language that matches the desired tone and style.
   - Use words that set the tone for the desired style of communication.

3. **Context Awareness:**
   - Provide relevant context to guide the model's understanding.
   - Include relevant information, keywords, or specific details.

4. **Avoiding Bias and Controversial Content:**
   - Be mindful of bias and controversial content in prompts.
   - Avoid biased language or offensive responses.
   - Ensure a balanced approach in prompts.

5. **Localization and Cultural Sensitivity:**
   - Consider the cultural context and language nuances.
   - Use appropriate language, idioms, and references that are relevant to the audience's culture and region

6. **Testing and Iterating Prompts for Improved Performance:**
   - A/B Testing: Conduct A/B testing with multiple prompts.
   - Prompt Variations: Experiment with different prompt variations.
   - Contextual Testing: Test prompts in different contextual scenarios.
   - Input Length Testing: Test prompts with varying input lengths.
   - Edge Case Testing: Test prompts with unique or challenging scenarios.

7. **Incorporating Feedback from AI Models to Refine Prompts:**
   - Analyze and interpret model outputs.
   - Identify areas of improvement in prompts.
   - Iterate and fine-tune prompts based on model feedback.
   - Continuously refine prompts for optimal performance.

CHAPTER 6

Practical Guide to ChatGPT APIs

In this chapter, the topics covered include:

- APIs and Their Functionalities
- API Interaction Methods
- Customizable API Parameters
- Temperature & Max Tokens
- API Limitations & Considerations
- Best Practices for API Integration
- Tips for Mastering ChatGPT APIs

✎ APIs and Their Functionalities

In today's interconnected digital world, software applications often need to communicate and interact with each other to exchange data and perform tasks. This is where Application Programming Interfaces (APIs) play a crucial role.

APIs act as a bridge between different software applications, allowing them to interact and share information in a standardized way. APIs define a set of rules and protocols that enable communication and data exchange between applications, making it possible for developers to build new functionalities on top of existing applications or integrate several applications seamlessly.

ChatGPT APIs, specifically, provide powerful capabilities for text generation and completion tasks. They enable developers to generate text based on prompts provided to the API, making it possible to generate creative content, complete sentences, or create conversational agents for various purposes.

The functionalities of ChatGPT APIs include:

1. **Text Generation**: ChatGPT APIs can generate text based on prompts provided to the API. This can include completing sentences, generating paragraphs, or creating entire articles, stories, and other types of text.

2. **Conversation Handling**: ChatGPT APIs can handle multi-turn conversations, allowing developers to create conversational agents that can carry out back-and-forth interactions with users. This can be useful for creating chatbots, virtual assistants, and customer service agents.

3. **Prompt Engineering**: ChatGPT APIs provide flexibility in crafting prompts to guide the model's output. Developers can experiment with different prompts, instructions, or parameters to obtain desired results, making prompt engineering essential to utilize ChatGPT APIs effectively.

4. **Customization**: Some ChatGPT APIs offer customization options, allowing developers to fine-tune the model for specific use cases or domains. This can enhance the model's performance and generate more relevant and accurate outputs.

5. **Language Support**: ChatGPT APIs support multiple languages, making them versatile for a wide range of applications and global audiences.

By leveraging the functionalities of ChatGPT APIs, developers can create a wide array of applications that generate text, complete sentences, and engage in interactive conversations with users, opening up endless possibilities for creative content generation, conversational experiences, customer service applications, and more.

# API Interaction Methods

Once you have a good understanding of the functionalities offered by ChatGPT APIs, the next step is to learn how to interact with these APIs to make requests and receive responses. ChatGPT APIs typically use standard protocols, like RESTful API calls, HTTP requests, and JSON payloads, for communication. Let us explore the different methods to interact with ChatGPT APIs and how to handle API requests and responses using popular programming languages.

1. **RESTful API Calls**: REST (Representational State Transfer) is a common architectural style used for designing networked applications. ChatGPT APIs may expose RESTful endpoints that you can call to send requests and receive responses. You can make RESTful API calls using HTTP methods such as GET, POST, PUT, DELETE, etc., to interact with ChatGPT APIs.

2. **HTTP Requests**: Another common method to interact with ChatGPT APIs is by sending HTTP requests directly. You can construct HTTP requests with the necessary headers, parameters, and payload to send to the API endpoint. This method allows for better flexibility in handling different types of requests and responses.

3. **JSON Payloads**: ChatGPT APIs typically expect and return data in JSON format. JSON (JavaScript Object Notation) is a lightweight data interchange format that is easy to read and write. You need to construct JSON payloads with the required data and key-value structure to send as input to the API and parse the JSON responses received from the API.

Handling API responses and errors is an essential part of working with ChatGPT APIs. Depending on the API and the programming language you are using, you can parse the API response to extract the relevant data or handle error codes appropriately.

🖥️ Key Customizable API Parameters

1. **Temperature**: This parameter controls the randomness of the responses generated by ChatGPT. A lower temperature value will result in more predictable and conservative responses, while a higher temperature value will lead to creative and diverse responses.

   Scenario: If a content developer is using ChatGPT to generate product descriptions, they may choose to use a low temperature value to ensure the descriptions remain consistent with the brand's messaging.

   A temperature of 0 will only generate the most likely response, while a temperature of 1 will allow for more diverse and surprising responses. A temperature value between 0.7 and 1 is ideal for generating creative and novel content.

2. **Tokens**: This parameter allows the user to specify certain tokens to be included or excluded from the generated responses. Tokens can be thought of as keywords or phrases that are relevant to the prompt.

   Scenario: If a retailer is using ChatGPT to generate responses to customer queries, they may include tokens such as "shipping," "returns," and "discounts" to ensure that the responses are focused on these specific topics.

3. **Top P**: This parameter controls the diversity of the responses generated. It specifies the probability mass that should be used for generating the next token in the sequence.

   Scenario: If a product manager is using ChatGPT to generate product names, they can use a higher Top P value to increase the diversity of the names generated by the model.

   Acceptable range for Top P is between 0 and 1, with a value of 1 indicating that all words are equally probable. A Top P value between 0.8 and 1 is recommended for generating diverse and engaging responses.

4. **Frequency Penalty**: This parameter encourages ChatGPT to generate responses that are more diverse by penalizing the model for repeating the same tokens in the generated responses.

   Scenario: If a marketing manager is using ChatGPT to generate an ad copy, they can use a higher Frequency Penalty value to encourage the model to generate a unique and diverse ad copy.

   Acceptable range for Frequency Penalty is between 0 and 1, with a higher value indicating a stronger penalty. A Frequency Penalty value of 0.5 is recommended for generating unique and varied responses.

5. **Presence Penalty**: This parameter encourages ChatGPT to generate responses that are more focused on the prompt by penalizing the model for including tokens that are not present in the prompt.

   Scenario: If an HR professional is using ChatGPT to generate job descriptions, they may use a higher Presence Penalty value to ensure that the generated descriptions are closely aligned with the job requirements outlined in the prompt.

   Acceptable range for Presence Penalty is between 0 and 1, with a higher value indicating a stronger penalty. A Presence Penalty value of 0.5 is recommended for generating responses that are distinct from the input prompt.

Impact of Temperature & Max Tokens

Temperature Token: Let us examine how Temperature tokens work with an illustrative prompt.

Prompt: *"Generate a product description for a new pair of running shoes."*

With Temperature = 0.8:

API Request: *"Temperature: 0.8, Max Tokens: 100"*

API Response: *"Introducing our cutting-edge running shoes! These high-performance sneakers feature advanced cushioning technology for unparalleled comfort, while the breathable mesh upper keeps your feet cool and dry. With their sleek design and superior traction, these shoes are perfect for both casual joggers and serious athletes. Get ready to up your running game with our innovative running shoes!"*

Max Tokens: Let us examine the impact of changing the max tokens with the above example.

Prompt: *"Generate a product description for a new pair of running shoes."*

With Max Tokens = 50:

API Request: *"Temperature: 0.5, Max Tokens: 50"*

API Response: *"Our latest running shoes are packed with advanced features to enhance your performance. The unbeatable comfort of cushioned sole and the lightweight design ensure a smooth and responsive stride. These shoes are perfect for runners of all levels, whether you are hitting the pavement or tackling trails. Experience the ultimate in running comfort and performance with our new running shoes!"*

When using ChatGPT APIs for prompt engineering tasks, experimentation with temperature and max tokens settings can help fine-tune the generated output to meet specific requirements and achieve the desired results. It may require trial and error to find the optimal values for these parameters depending on the specific use case and desired outcomes.

API Limitations & Considerations

ChatGPT APIs offer powerful capabilities for generating human-like text, but it is important to be aware of their limitations and considerations when using them in prompt engineering. Here are some key points to keep in mind:

1. **Potential Biases**: Like any language model, ChatGPT APIs may have biases embedded in their training data, which can result in biased responses. It is important to be mindful of potential biases in the generated content and carefully review and evaluate the model's output to ensure it aligns with ethical and inclusive principles. Prompt engineering can help mitigate biases by providing explicit instructions to avoid biased or discriminatory content.

2. **Sensitivity to Input Phrasing**: ChatGPT APIs can be sensitive to the phrasing and wording of prompts. Minor changes in phrasing can yield different results, and the model may not always ask clarifying questions for ambiguous queries. It is crucial to be precise and explicit in your prompts to get the desired output. Experimenting with prompt styles and wording can help optimize the model's responses.

3. **Need for Careful Prompt Engineering**: The quality of your prompts plays a crucial role in the accuracy and relevance of the model's responses. Crafting effective prompts requires trial and error, experimentation, and iterative refinement. Carefully consider the desired outcome and provide clear, specific, and context-rich prompts to guide the model towards generating the desired content.

4. **Ethical Use, Data Privacy, and Compliance**: When using ChatGPT APIs, it is important to adhere to ethical principles and legal requirements. Be mindful of the content generated by the model and ensure it complies with data privacy regulations, intellectual property rights, and other legal considerations. Follow OpenAI's usage policies and guidelines to ensure responsible and compliant use of APIs.

5. **Model Limitations**: ChatGPT APIs are powerful language models, but they have their limitations. They may not always provide accurate or reliable answers, especially for complex or ambiguous queries. The model's responses should be carefully evaluated and

validated, and human oversight may be necessary for critical applications.

6. **Rapid API Changes**: APIs are subject to updates and modifications, and ChatGPT APIs may evolve. Stay updated with the latest API documentation, guidelines, and announcements from OpenAI, to ensure you are using up-to-date features and functionalities.

7. **Computational Resources and Costs**: Generating text with ChatGPT APIs requires computational resources and may incur costs based on API usage. Be mindful of the resources consumed and the associated costs. Optimize your API calls and usage to stay within your budget and resource limits.

Best Practices for API Integration

Integrating ChatGPT APIs into your applications requires careful consideration of numerous factors, including scalability, performance, security, and cost optimization. Here are some of the best practices to follow:

1. **Scalability**: Design your integration to handle scalable API usage and traffic. Consider factors such as concurrent requests, response time, and resource utilization. Optimize your code and architecture to ensure efficient handling of API calls and minimize potential performance bottlenecks.

2. **Performance**: Optimize the performance of your API calls by minimizing unnecessary requests, leveraging batch processing where possible, and optimizing parameters such as temperature and max tokens to control the output length and quality. Experiment with different settings to find the right balance between response time and quality of generated content.

3. **Security**: Follow the best practices for securing your API integration, including proper management of API credentials, authentication, and authorization. Use HTTPS for secure communication, encrypt sensitive data, and implement appropriate authentication

mechanisms to ensure that only authorized users can access the API. Regularly review and update your security measures to protect against potential vulnerabilities.

4. **Monitoring**: Monitor your API usage to track performance, identify and resolve issues, and optimize costs. Utilize logging, monitoring, and analytics tools to gain insights into API usage patterns, error rates, and resource utilization. This can help you identify and address potential performance bottlenecks, optimize costs, and improve the overall user experience.

5. **Cost Optimization**: Be mindful of the costs associated with API usage and optimize your API calls to stay within budget. Avoid unnecessary API calls, optimize input, and output parameters to control usage, and utilize OpenAI's pricing and billing resources to understand and manage your costs effectively.

6. **Credential and Authentication Management**: Effectively manage and protect your API credentials and authentication tokens. Store sensitive information securely, restrict access to authorized personnel only, and follow best practices for credential rotation and management. Implement appropriate authentication mechanisms, such as OAuth, to ensure secure and authorized access to the APIs.

Mastering ChatGPT APIs

1. **Craft Clear and Specific Prompts**: The quality of your prompts plays a crucial role in getting accurate and relevant responses from ChatGPT. Be clear and specific in your prompts, clearly stating your desired outcome or question. Avoid ambiguous or vague prompts that can lead to ambiguous or irrelevant responses.

2. **Experiment with Parameters**: ChatGPT APIs allow you to tweak parameters such as temperature and max tokens to control the output. Experiment with different values to find the optimal settings for your use case. Higher temperature values (e.g., 0.8) result in more random and creative responses, while lower values (e.g.,

0.2) produce more focused and deterministic responses. Adjusting max tokens can limit the length of the response.

3. **Manage Conversation History:** If you are working with multi-turn conversations, it is important to manage the conversation history properly. Include the entire conversation history, including user and ChatGPT responses, as part of the input to maintain context. You can use system-level instructions to guide the model's behavior in the conversation. Be mindful of the token limit and truncate or omit less relevant parts if needed.

4. **Test and Iterate**: Experiment with different prompts, parameters, and conversation flows to fine-tune the results. Test your prompts and API calls thoroughly to understand the model's behavior and ensure desired outcomes. Iterate and refine your prompts based on the model's responses to improve the quality of the conversation.

5. **Implement Error Handling Strategies**: ChatGPT APIs may return errors or incomplete responses in certain scenarios. Implement effective error-handling strategies in your code to handle potential issues, such as timeouts, rate limits, or unexpected errors. Proper error handling will ensure smooth and reliable integration of ChatGPT APIs into your applications or workflows.

6. **Stay Updated with API Changes**: Keep yourself updated with any changes or updates to the ChatGPT API documentation, guidelines, or terms of use. Stay informed about any updates or improvements to the API to ensure you are utilizing the latest features and functionalities.

7. **Follow OpenAI's Usage Policies**: It is important to adhere to OpenAI's usage policies and guidelines when utilizing ChatGPT APIs. Familiarize yourself with the terms of service, usage limitations, and ethical considerations outlined by OpenAI to ensure responsible and ethical use of the API.

By following these tips, you can effectively utilize ChatGPT APIs in real-world prompt engineering scenarios and create engaging and dynamic conversations with the model, tailored to your needs and requirements.

💡 Tips for Getting the Most Out of API Responses

1. **Start with a Clear Objective**: Before using the ChatGPT API, it is crucial to define your objective clearly. Outline the specific task or problem you want the API to help you with, whether it is generating content, providing recommendations, or answering questions. Having a well-defined objective helps in designing appropriate prompts and instructions to get desired results.

2. **Iterate and Experiment**: Experimentation is key to optimizing the performance of ChatGPT APIs. Do not be afraid to iterate and experiment with different prompts, instructions, and parameters to fine-tune the model's responses according to your requirements. You can iterate and experiment with various prompt engineering techniques, input formats, and parameters such as Temperature, Max Tokens, Presence Penalty, Frequency Penalty, etc., to improve output quality and relevance.

◎ Chapter Summary

In this chapter, we have explored the capabilities of ChatGPT APIs.

- APIs act as a bridge between software applications, allowing them to communicate and share information in a standardized way.

- ChatGPT APIs provide functionalities such as text generation, conversation handling, prompt engineering, customization, and language support.

- Interaction with ChatGPT APIs can be done through RESTful API calls, HTTP requests, and JSON payloads.

- Multiple tunable API concepts like Temperature, Max Tokens, Performance Tokens, Penalty Tokens, and Top P help in improving prompt effectiveness and diversity of responses.

- Tips for mastering ChatGPT APIs include crafting clear and specific prompts, experimenting with parameters, managing conversation history, testing and iterating, implementing error-handling strategies, and staying updated with API-related changes.

CHAPTER 7

Sentiment Analysis with ChatGPT

Sentiment analysis involves using Natural Language Processing techniques to analyze text data and determine the sentiment of the writer. It can be used by businesses to gain valuable insights into customer feedback and employee engagement. It is a widely used tool in various industry segments and ChatGPT is a very handy tool to do sentiment analysis on a regular basis to enhance the quality of service, deliver new features or functionality, or improve employee engagement levels.

✎ Here are four specific examples of how sentiment analysis can be used:

1. **Retail Industry**: A clothing retailer wants to analyze customer reviews to understand their overall satisfaction and identify areas for improvement. The retailer can use sentiment analysis to determine the sentiment of the reviews and identify common themes. Prompts for this use case could include:

   Prompt 1: *"Analyze customer reviews of our clothing line to determine overall sentiment and identify areas for improvement."*

   Prompt 2: *"What are customers saying about our customer service? Analyze reviews to identify common themes and sentiments."*

2. **Product Insight**: A consumer goods company wants to analyze social media posts to gain insight into how consumers are using their products and what features they like or dislike. The company can use sentiment analysis to identify the sentiment of the

posts and extract relevant insights. Prompts for this use case could include:

Prompt 1: *"Analyze social media posts related to our new product launch to understand customer sentiments and identify features that are resonating with customers."*

Prompt 2: *"What are customers saying about our competitor's product? Analyze social media posts to gain insight into consumer sentiments and preferences."*

3. **Employee Engagement Survey Data**: A company wants to analyze the results of an employee engagement survey to understand how employees feel about their workplace and identify areas for improvement. The company can use sentiment analysis to determine the sentiment of the responses and extract relevant insights. Prompts for this use case could include:

Prompt 1: *"Analyze employee survey responses to determine overall sentiment and identify areas for improvement."*

Prompt 2: *"What are employees saying about our company culture? Analyze survey responses to identify common themes and sentiments."*

4. **Social Media Monitoring**: Sentiment analysis can be used for social media monitoring and reputation management. By analyzing the sentiment of social media posts and comments, companies can quickly identify and address any negative feedback or concerns that customers may have. They can also use sentiment analysis to track their brand's reputation over time and make informed decisions about marketing and customer service strategies.

Let us examine some specific examples of social media monitoring and reputation management:

Social Media Monitoring:

Use case 1: A company wants to monitor customer sentiment on Twitter to gauge overall satisfaction with its brand and identify any areas for improvement.

Prompt 1: *"What are customers saying about our brand on Twitter?"*

Use case 2: A marketing team wants to stay up to date on the latest trends in their industry by monitoring popular hashtags being used on Instagram.

Prompt 2: *"What are the top hashtags being used in our industry on Instagram?"*

Reputation Management:

Use case 1: A company wants to identify common issues or complaints with their product on Amazon and take steps to address them to improve their overall reputation.

Prompt 1: *"What are the top negative reviews about our product on Amazon?"*

Use case 2: A company wants to monitor their online reputation by keeping track of customer reviews on popular review websites and addressing any negative feedback.

Prompt 2: *"What are people saying about our brand on consumer review websites like Yelp and Google Reviews?"*

Baseline Data for Sentiment Analysis

Let us explore how to do write effective prompts for a restaurant brand name called "Tasty Bites".

Prompt: You are a social media manager for Tasty Bites, a restaurant chain. Your task is to monitor the sentiment of the Tasty Bites brand on social media platforms. Use sentiment analysis to determine the overall sentiment of the Tasty Bites brand and identify any trends in sentiment over time.

Social media platforms: Suppose the sentiment analysis will be conducted on Twitter and Instagram. The prompt would be modified as:

Prompt: You are a social media manager for Tasty Bites, a restaurant chain. Your task is to monitor the sentiment of the Tasty Bites brand on Twitter and Instagram. Use sentiment analysis to determine the overall sentiment of the Tasty Bites brand and identify any trends in sentiment over time.

Timeframe: Let's say the sentiment analysis should cover the past month. The prompt would be adjusted as:

Prompt: You are a social media manager for Tasty Bites, a restaurant chain. Your task is to monitor the sentiment of the Tasty Bites brand on social media platforms over the past month. Use sentiment analysis to determine the overall sentiment of the Tasty Bites brand and identify any trends in sentiment over time.

Relevant keywords: Suppose common keywords associated with Tasty Bites are "delicious food," "excellent service," and "friendly staff." The prompt would include these keywords as:

Prompt: You are a social media manager for Tasty Bites, a restaurant chain. Your task is to monitor the sentiment of the Tasty Bites brand on social media platforms. Use sentiment analysis to determine the overall sentiment of the Tasty Bites brand and identify any trends in sentiment over time. Focus on keywords like "delicious food," "excellent service," and "friendly staff" to capture customer sentiments accurately.

By incorporating these additional details into the prompt, the sentiment analysis can be tailored to the specific brand, social media platforms, timeframe, and relevant keywords, allowing for more precise monitoring of sentiment and trend analysis.

Data Filters in Sentiment Analysis

Data filters in sentiment analysis refer to techniques and criteria used to refine and extract relevant data from a larger dataset for sentiment analysis purposes. These filters help eliminate noise, focus on specific aspects, and enhance the accuracy and quality of sentiment analysis results.

Outlined below are some important considerations that need to be considered in applying data filters:

1. Remove Noise: Cleanse the data by removing irrelevant or noisy content such as advertisements, spam, or irrelevant user comments.

2. Filter by Relevance: Focus on relevant data by filtering out non-essential information. This can be done by setting criteria based on keywords, specific platforms, or relevant time frames.

3. Exclude Neutral Sentiments: Depending on the analysis goal, it may be useful to exclude neutral sentiment data points to concentrate on positive or negative sentiments. This helps in obtaining more focused insights.

4. Consider User Influence: Consider the influence of users in the sentiment analysis. For example, you may want to prioritize comments from verified customers or influential individuals for a more accurate analysis.

5. Handle Language Variations: If your brand operates in multiple languages or regions, consider using language-specific filters to focus on sentiment analysis for specific markets.

Best Practices in Sentiment Analysis

1. **Choose the Right Model**: It is important to choose the right ChatGPT model for your specific use case. Some models may be more accurate for certain types of sentiment analysis than others.

   Here are some model options to consider:

   Base ChatGPT Model: The base ChatGPT model can be used for general sentiment analysis tasks. It provides a good starting point for analyzing sentiment in text, offering a balance between accuracy and versatility. It is suitable for a wide range of applications where sentiment understanding is required.

   Fine-tuned Sentiment Analysis Models: Some ChatGPT models are specifically fine-tuned for sentiment analysis tasks. These models have undergone additional training to specialize in understanding and analyzing sentiment. They are often trained on sentiment-labeled datasets, enabling them to provide more accurate and nuanced sentiment analysis results compared to the base model.

Domain-Specific Sentiment Analysis Models: Depending on your industry or specific domain, there may be sentiment analysis models fine-tuned specifically for that domain. These models are trained on domain-specific data and can offer better performance and accuracy when analyzing sentiment within that particular context. For example, there might be models fine-tuned for sentiment analysis in finance, healthcare, or e-commerce.

Large-scale Models: Some sentiment analysis tasks require processing large volumes of data or dealing with complex sentiments. In such cases, using larger and more powerful ChatGPT models, such as those with higher token limits or enhanced language understanding capabilities, can be beneficial. These models can handle more extensive text inputs and provide more comprehensive sentiment analysis results.

2. **Use a Large and Diverse Dataset**: The quality of the training data used to train the model has a significant impact on the accuracy of the results. It is important to use a large and diverse dataset that covers a range of topics and emotions.

3. **Preprocess Your Data**: Preprocessing your data can help to improve the accuracy of the sentiment analysis. This includes tasks such as removing stop words, stemming, and lemmatization.

4. **Fine-Tune the Model**: Fine-tuning the ChatGPT model can help to improve the accuracy of the results. This involves training the model on your specific dataset to make it more accurate for your use case.

5. **Validate the Results**: It is important to validate the results of the sentiment analysis to ensure that they are accurate. This can be done through a manual review of a sample of the data or using a separate dataset for validation.

6. **Monitor the Performance**: Monitoring the performance of the sentiment analysis over time can help to identify any issues or changes in

the accuracy of the results. This can be done by periodically reviewing the results and adjusting the model as needed.

7. **Consider the Context**: It is important to consider the context in which the sentiment analysis is being used. The same sentiment may have different meanings in different contexts, so it is important to take this into account when interpreting the results.

8. **Continuously Improve**: Sentiment analysis is not a one-time task, but an ongoing process. It is important to continuously monitor and improve the accuracy of the results over time.

Lab Exercises

In this lab exercise, you will have the opportunity to gain hands-on experience with sentiment analysis. You will work on five use cases, ranging from low to moderate to challenging difficulty levels. Each use case will provide you with an opportunity to explore different ways in which sentiment analysis can be applied to real-world scenarios.

In each of the use cases, you will need to select a dataset and apply appropriate techniques to perform sentiment analysis. You will then need to analyze the results and provide insights based on your analysis.

Use Case 1: Social Media Monitoring (Low Difficulty Level)

You are a social media manager for a restaurant chain. Your task is to monitor the sentiment of the brand on social media platforms. Write a prompt to use sentiment analysis to determine the overall sentiment of the brand and identify any trends in sentiment over time.

Use Case 2: Product Reviews (Low to Moderate Difficulty Level)

You are a product manager for an e-commerce company. Your task is to analyze customer reviews of your company's products. Write a prompt to use sentiment analysis to determine the overall sentiment of the reviews and identify any specific areas for improvement.

<u>*Use Case 3*</u>: Reputation Management (Moderate Difficulty Level)

You are a public relations manager for a tech company. Your task is to monitor the sentiment of media coverage of the company and its products. Write a prompt to use sentiment analysis to determine the overall sentiment of the coverage and identify any potential reputation management issues.

<u>*Use Case 4*</u>: Customer Service (Moderate to Challenging Difficulty Level)

You are a customer service manager for a telecommunications company. Your task is to analyze customer feedback to improve the customer experience. Write a prompt to use sentiment analysis to determine the overall sentiment of customer feedback and identify any specific issues that customers are experiencing.

<u>*Use Case 5*</u>: Employee Engagement Survey (Challenging Difficulty Level)

You are an HR manager for a large corporation. Your task is to analyze the results of the annual employee engagement survey. Write a prompt to use sentiment analysis to determine the overall sentiment of the survey responses and identify any specific areas of concern.

CHAPTER 8

Challenges in Prompt Engineering

In this chapter, the topics covered include:

- Addressing Common Challenges & Pitfalls
- Strategies for Improving Prompt Effectiveness
- Ethical Considerations in Prompt Engineering

Addressing Common Challenges & Pitfalls

Prompt engineering, like any other Natural Language Processing task, can come with its own set of challenges and pitfalls. Some common challenges include:

1. **Ambiguity**: Example of an ambiguous prompt: *"Write a story about a dog."* This prompt is vague and lacks specificity, leaving room for the model to interpret the desired story in different ways. The output could be a story about a cute pet dog or a story about a stray dog causing trouble. The ambiguity in the prompt can lead to varied outputs that may not align with the desired intent.

   Improved prompt: *"Write a heartwarming story about a loyal Labrador Retriever who helps a young girl find her way back home in a snowstorm."* This prompt provides specific details about the desired story, including the genre, details of the protagonist, and plot, which reduce ambiguity and guide the model towards generating a more aligned output.

2. **Bias:** Example of a biased prompt: *"Write a review of a rom-com movie, but focus on how funny the male lead is."* This prompt contains biased language that favors the male lead and may result in a biased output that downplays the female characters or perpetuates gender stereotypes.

    Improved prompt: *"Write an unbiased review of a rom-com movie, focusing on the chemistry between the lead characters and the humor in the plot."* This prompt removes biased language and emphasizes an unbiased review, guiding the model towards generating a more balanced and fair output.

3. **Lack of Clarity:** Example of a vague prompt: *"Design a logo for a fashion brand."* This prompt lacks clarity and does not provide specific guidance on the desired logo design, leading to potential misinterpretation by the model.

    Improved prompt: *"Design a minimalist logo for a high-end fashion brand with a modern and timeless look, incorporating the brand name and a subtle reference to a fashion accessory like a pearl necklace."* This prompt provides clear and specific instructions on the desired logo design, including the style, elements, and references, which helps the model generate an aligned output.

4. **Over-Specification:** Example of an overly specific prompt: *"Write a poem about a rose with 5 stanzas, each with 4 lines, and use the words 'red,' 'fragrance,' 'petals,' and 'thorns' in every stanza."* This prompt overly dictates the structure and content of the poem, leaving little room for creativity or diversity in the output.

    Improved prompt: *"Write a poem that captures the beauty and symbolism of a rose, incorporating the words 'red,' 'fragrance,' 'petals,' and 'thorns' in a way that evokes emotion and imagery."* This prompt provides guidance on the desired theme and words to include, while allowing the model to have creative freedom in generating the poem.

5. **Length Constraints**: Example of a prompt that is too short: *"Describe a sunset."* This prompt is too short and lacks sufficient information, making it challenging for the model to understand the intended task and generate meaningful output.

   Improved prompt: *"Write a vivid and sensory description of a breathtaking sunset over the ocean, including the colors, clouds, reflections, and the emotions it evokes."* This prompt provides more details and context, helping the model to better understand the desired description and generate a rich and engaging output.

6. **Iterative Refinement**: Example of an initial prompt: *"Write a story about a mysterious island."* After testing the model's responses, it's identified that the outputs lack the desired level of suspense and intrigue.

   Refined prompt: *"Write a gripping adventure story about a group of explorers who stumble upon an uncharted island with ancient ruins and a hidden treasure, but soon realize they are not alone and must uncover the island's secrets to survive."* This refined prompt incorporates the feedback from the model's initial responses and provides specific instructions to guide the model towards the desired output.

7. **Conflicting Instructions**: Example of a prompt with conflicting instructions: *"Write a poem about love without using any romantic words."* This prompt presents conflicting instructions as it asks for a poem about love, while prohibiting the use of romantic words, creating confusion for the model.

   Improved prompt: *"Write a poem that conveys the essence of love using non-romantic words and metaphors."* This prompt clarifies the desired intent and provides a coherent instruction, guiding the model towards generating a more aligned output.

8. **Incomplete Information**: Example of a prompt with incomplete information: *"Create a recipe for a dish."* This prompt lacks critical information such as the type of dish, main ingredients, or cooking

instructions, making it challenging for the model to generate a complete recipe.

Improved prompt: *"Create a recipe for a delicious and healthy chicken stir-fry with colorful vegetables, including the list of ingredients, step-by-step cooking instructions, and serving suggestions."* This prompt provides comprehensive information on the desired dish, helping the model to generate a complete and well-structured recipe.

9. **Lack of Constraints**: Example of a prompt without constraints: *"Design a logo for a company."* This prompt does not specify any constraints or limitations, leaving the model with unlimited possibilities, which may result in impractical or irrelevant outputs.

Improved prompt: *"Design a simple and elegant logo for a technology company that incorporates the colors blue and silver, with a focus on modernity and innovation."* This prompt establishes constraints in terms of design elements, colors, and overall style, guiding the model towards generating a relevant and aligned logo.

10. **Unclear Expectations**: Example of a prompt with unclear expectations: *"Write a news article about a recent event."* This prompt does not specify the tone, format, or specific event, leaving the model with unclear expectations, which may result in an output that does not meet the desired intent.

Improved prompt: *"Write an objective news article in a formal tone about the recent United Nations Climate Change Summit, highlighting the key discussions, outcomes, and implications."* This prompt provides clear expectations in terms of tone, format, and specific event, helping the model to generate an accurate and aligned news article.

Remember that prompt engineering is an iterative process, and continuous refinement of prompts based on model responses and feedback is essential to achieve desired outputs.

 Strategies for Improving Prompt Effectiveness

Here are some strategies that can help enhance the effectiveness of prompts:

1. **Clarity and Specificity**: Make sure your prompts are clear, specific, and leave no room for ambiguity. Clearly state what you want the model to do or provide, and specify any constraints, formatting, or requirements.

   Instead of *"Write a story about a dog,"* use *"Write a heartwarming short story about a loyal Labrador Retriever who helps a young girl find her way back home after getting lost in the woods."*

2. **Context and Background information**: Provide sufficient context and relevant background information in your prompts to help the model better understand the task or problem at hand. This can include details such as relevant dates, names, locations, or any other relevant information.

   Instead of *"Write a product review,"* use *"Write a detailed product review of the XYZ smartwatch, highlighting its features, performance, battery life, and compatibility with iOS and Android devices."*

3. **Constraints and Limitations**: Establish clear constraints and limitations in your prompts to guide the model towards generating more realistic and aligned outputs. This can include specifying word limits, required elements, or desired style.

   Instead of *"Design a logo for a restaurant,"* use *"Design a minimalist logo for a vegan restaurant that incorporates green and earthy tones, and does not include any animal-related images."*

4. **Instructional Language**: Use clear and concise instructional language in your prompts, and consider using imperative verbs or step-by-step instructions to guide the model towards desired actions.

Instead of *"What are some benefits of exercise?"* use *"List five key benefits of regular exercise, providing a brief description for each."*

5. **Feedback-Based Refinement**: Continuously iterate and refine your prompts based on the model's responses and feedback. Experiment with different prompts and learn from the model's outputs to optimize your prompts for better effectiveness.

   After receiving outputs from the model, analyze the results and identify areas for improvement. Adjust your prompts accordingly to address any issues or gaps in the model's responses.

6. **Domain-Specific Prompts**: Consider using prompts that are tailored to the specific domain or task you are working on. Domain-specific prompts can provide the model with the necessary context and guidance to generate relevant and accurate outputs.

   Instead of *"Write a news article,"* use *"Write a news article on the recent advancements in renewable energy technology, highlighting the impact on the environment, economy, and future prospects."*

By employing these strategies, you can optimize your prompts to effectively guide the model towards generating desired outputs and achieving your intended results. Remember to experiment, iterate, and refine your prompts based on the model's responses to continuously improve their effectiveness.

Ethical Considerations in Prompt Engineering

As with any technology, the use of language models like ChatGPT raises ethical concerns that should be taken into account. Here are some key ethical considerations to keep in mind when engaging in prompt engineering:

1. **Bias and Fairness**: Language models can inadvertently learn biases from the data they are trained on, which can result in biased outputs. It's important to be mindful of potential biases in prompts

and avoid reinforcing or amplifying existing biases. Take steps to ensure fairness and inclusivity in the prompts you create.

Avoid using prompts that reinforce stereotypes or discriminatory language, and strive to create prompts that promote diversity and inclusivity in the model's responses.

2. **Misinformation and Disinformation**: Language models can generate outputs that may contain misinformation or disinformation. Be cautious with prompts that could potentially lead to the creation of false or misleading information. Avoid using prompts that may encourage the model to generate inaccurate or harmful content.

    For instance, avoid prompts that ask the model to create fake news articles, misleading information, or harmful content that could spread misinformation.

3. **Privacy and Data Protection**: Language models may inadvertently generate outputs that contain private or sensitive information. Be cautious with prompts that may ask the model to generate personal, confidential, or sensitive data. Respect user privacy and ensure compliance with relevant data protection regulations.

    For example, avoid prompts that ask the model to generate personal identification numbers (PINs), passwords, financial information, or any other sensitive data.

4. **Consent and User Awareness**: Language models may generate outputs that users may not have explicitly consented to or may not be aware of. Be transparent about the use of language models and obtain user consent wherever necessary. Inform users about the potential generation of content by language models and how it may be used.

    Disclose the use of language models in any application or platform that utilizes their outputs, and ensure that users are aware of the generated content and its potential implications.

5. **Unintended Consequences**: Prompt engineering may have unintended consequences, such as generating outputs that are unexpected or undesirable. Be mindful of the potential impact of prompt engineering and carefully consider the ethical implications of the generated content.

   Avoid prompts that may result in outputs that are offensive, harmful, or could have unintended consequences, such as promoting violence, discrimination, or illegal activities.

6. **Transparency and Accountability**: It's important to be transparent and accountable for the prompts that are used to guide language models. Document and disclose the prompts that are used, and take responsibility for the content that is generated as a result of prompt engineering.

   Keep a record of the prompts used in your experiments and provide clear attribution and accountability for the generated content.

By taking into account these ethical considerations in prompt engineering, you can ensure responsible and ethical use of language models like ChatGPT, and mitigate potential risks or unintended consequences associated with their outputs. Remember to always prioritize fairness, accuracy, privacy, consent, and accountability in your prompt engineering practices.

◎ Chapter Summary

To improve the effectiveness of prompts in prompt engineering, remember to:

- Be specific and clear: Provide clear and specific instructions in the prompts to guide the model towards generating desired outputs. Avoid ambiguous language or overly broad prompts that leave room for misinterpretation.

- Avoid bias: Ensure that prompts do not contain biased language or instructions that favor certain perspectives or perpetuate stereotypes. Use inclusive and unbiased language to promote fairness and diversity in the generated outputs.

- Strike a balance between over-specification and lack of constraints: Provide enough guidance to direct the model towards desired outputs, but also allow for creativity and diversity. Avoid overly dictating the structure, content, or style, as it may limit the model's creativity.

- Incorporate iterative refinement: Continuously iterate and refine prompts based on the model's responses to narrow the gap between the purpose of the prompts and the generated outputs. Analyze the generated outputs and provide feedback to refine prompts and make them more effective.

- Consider ethical considerations: Ensure that prompts do not violate ethical guidelines, such as promoting hate speech, discrimination, or other unethical behaviors. Consider the potential impact of generated outputs and design prompts accordingly.

Prompt Engineering Cookbooks

📝 Prompt Cookbook for Content Marketers

Content Marketers often face challenges in generating engaging taglines, product descriptions, and other creative content. Overcome these challenges by leveraging ChatGPT's powerful capabilities to quickly generate unique and compelling content. Save time, streamline brainstorming, and captivate your audience with professional quality content.

Keep in mind that search engines like Google can punish websites that rely wholly on content generated by generative AI tools like ChatGPT and push your search rankings down. Use the tool for researching ideas, coming up with main topic points, researching topics, and reviewing your final draft. It should not become a substitute for human creativity.

Here is a cookbook of 12 useful prompts for content marketers:

1. Blog Post Idea Generator: *"Generate blog post ideas related to [topic/keyword] for [target audience]."*

2. Social Media Caption Generator: *"Generate catchy captions for social media posts promoting [product/service] to [target audience]."*

3. Headline Generator: *"Generate attention-grabbing headlines for articles about [topic/keyword] for [target audience]."*

4. Content Calendar Planner: *"Create a content calendar for [month/year] with topics, keywords, and publishing dates for [target audience]."*

5. Content Gap Analysis: *"Identify content gaps in the [industry/niche] for [target audience] and generate content ideas to fill those gaps."*

6. Keyword Research Assistant: *"Generate a list of relevant keywords for [topic/industry] to optimize content for search engine rankings."*

7. Call-to-Action (CTA) Generator: *"Generate effective CTAs for landing pages, blog posts, and social media posts to encourage user engagement."*

8. Email Newsletter Template: *"Design an email newsletter template with engaging content and visuals for [target audience]."*

9. Video Script Generator: *"Generate video script ideas for [topic/keyword] to create engaging video content for [target audience]."*

10. Content Repurposing Ideas: *"Generate creative ideas to repurpose existing content into different formats (e.g., infographics, podcasts, webinars) for [target audience]."*

11. Facebook Ad Copy Generator: *"Generate compelling ad copy for a Facebook ad campaign promoting [product/service] to [target audience]."*

12. TikTok Content Challenge Generator: *"Generate creative content and challenge ideas for TikTok videos related to [topic/keyword] to engage with [target audience]."*

These prompts can serve as a starting point for content marketers to generate a variety of content ideas, optimize their content for search engine rankings, create engaging social media posts, plan their content calendar, and more.

🔍 Prompt Cookbook for Marketing Managers

Marketing managers can harness the powerful Natural Language Processing capabilities of ChatGPT to streamline content creation, enhance customer engagement, and optimize overall marketing strategies.

Here is a cookbook of ready-to-use prompts for marketing managers.

1. Brand-Building Campaign: *"Design a brand-building campaign that includes a mix of online and offline marketing channels to increase brand awareness among [target audience]."*

2. Top-of-the-Funnel Content Strategy: *"Develop a content strategy to generate awareness and interest among [target audience] through blog posts, social media, and other content marketing efforts."*

3. Key Performance Indicators (KPIs) Tracking: *"Create a dashboard to track key marketing metrics, such as website traffic, social media engagement, and lead generation, to measure the effectiveness of marketing campaigns."*

4. Influencer Partnership: *"Identify and reach out to relevant influencers in [niche/industry] to collaborate on a brand partnership to expand brand reach and awareness."*

5. Social Media Campaign: *"Design and execute a social media campaign on platforms like Instagram or LinkedIn to drive brand awareness, engagement, and website traffic."*

6. Thought Leadership Strategy: *"Develop a thought leadership strategy that includes guest blogging, speaking engagements, and industry insights to establish [your brand] as a leader in the industry."*

7. Content Distribution Strategy: *"Create a content distribution strategy that includes a mix of organic and paid channels to amplify brand content and reach a wider audience."*

8. Brand Perception Research: *"Conduct a brand perception research study to gather insights on how [your target audience] perceives [your brand] and use the findings to inform brand-building strategies."*

9. Brand Messaging Framework: *"Develop a comprehensive brand messaging framework that includes key brand attributes, value proposition, and brand tone to ensure consistent messaging across all marketing efforts."*

10. Competitive Analysis: *"Conduct a thorough competitive analysis to identify the strengths and weaknesses of competitors' marketing strategies and leverage the insights to improve brand-building and awareness efforts."*

These prompts can provide marketing managers with actionable ideas to develop effective marketing strategies, measure key metrics, and build a strong brand presence in the market.

As a Product Manager's secret weapon, AI Models like ChatGPT empower them to ideate, prototype, and iterate product concepts faster than ever before. By leveraging its natural language capabilities. It can also aid in creating compelling product messaging and copywriting, optimizing user interfaces, and refining user experiences, making it a must-have tool for Product Managers looking to excel in product development and driving customer engagement.

Here is a cookbook of ready-to-use prompts for Product Managers that cover the entire product lifecycle:

Ideation and Market Research:

During the early stages of the product lifecycle, prompts can be used to gather insights and spark innovative ideas. Prompt AI models with questions like, "What are the emerging customer needs in our target market?" or "Which features are most desired by our potential customers?" Use the generated responses to inform your product ideation and market research efforts.

Competitive Analysis:

Stay ahead of the competition by leveraging prompts to analyze competitor moves. Prompt AI models to provide insights on competitor strategies, new product launches, or market positioning. For example, ask, "What are the key strengths and weaknesses of our main competitor's latest product?" Use these insights to refine your own product strategy and identify areas of differentiation.

Customer Feedback and Product Enhancement:

Prompt engineering can be a game-changer when it comes to gathering customer feedback and improving product features. Use prompts to ask AI models about customer pain points, feature preferences, or suggestions for improvement. For instance, ask, "What are the top three areas where our customers find our product challenging to use?"

Incorporate these insights into your product roadmap and prioritize enhancements accordingly.

Trend Tracking and Market Intelligence:

Keep a pulse on industry trends and market dynamics by using prompts to generate insights. Ask AI models about emerging technologies, market disruptions, or consumer preferences. Prompt with questions like, "What are the key trends shaping our industry in the next five years?" Use the generated information to inform your product strategy, identify new market opportunities, and make informed business decisions.

Iterative Testing and Validation:

As you iterate on your product, prompts can help validate assumptions and gather feedback at each stage. Prompt AI models with user scenarios, specific use cases, or hypothetical product interactions. Ask for feedback on usability, functionality, or potential issues. Use the generated responses to refine your product design and validate its alignment with user needs and expectations.

Effective Participation in Sprint Review Cycles:

Product Managers can leverage AI Models to enhance their effectiveness in Sprint Review Cycles. Utilize ChatGPT to aid in activities like storyboarding, prioritizing the product backlog, and identifying potential risks or dependencies. Use Prompts like "Suggest an optimal user story sequence for the upcoming sprint," "Identify any critical dependencies that may impact the sprint timeline," or "Recommend the top three features to prioritize in the product backlog based on customer feedback and market trends".

Sales Training and Product Launch:

Product managers can leverage ChatGPT to create interactive sales training materials prior to product launch. Prompt AI models with common customer objections, competitor comparisons, and key product features. Use the generated responses to develop sales scripts,

FAQs, and training modules. This empowers the sales team with accurate and up-to-date information, enabling them to effectively communicate the value proposition of the product to potential customers.

Product Documentation:

ChatGPT can be a valuable tool for product managers in creating comprehensive product documentation. Prompt AI models with specific questions about product functionality, integration processes, or troubleshooting steps. Use the generated responses to develop user manuals, technical guides, and knowledge bases. This ensures that customers and internal stakeholders have access to clear and accurate documentation, facilitating product adoption and reducing support overheads.

Here are some additional thoughts on how to use the prompts effectively for product life cycle management.

- Be specific in your prompts. The more specific you are, the better the results will be. For example, instead of asking "What are some new features that would make our product more user-friendly?", you could ask "What are some new features that would make it easier for customers to find the information they need?"

- Use keywords. When you're writing your prompts, use keywords that are relevant to your product or service. For example, if you're selling a software product, you might use keywords like "software", "productivity", and "efficiency".

- Experiment with different prompts. Don't be afraid to experiment with different prompts to see what works best. You may find that some prompts generate better results than others.

- Be patient. It may take some time to get the hang of using prompts. Don't get discouraged if you don't get the results, you want right away. Just keep experimenting and you'll eventually find what works for you.

⌨️ Prompt Cookbook for Project Managers

ChatGPT can serve as a valuable virtual project manager and a co-pilot throughout the project management lifecycle. Here is a cookbook of 15 ready-to-use prompts across the project lifecycle, that focus on the most common use cases:

1. **Project Initiation**

   Prompt: *"What are the key activities and deliverables needed during project initiation? Provide a checklist or template to ensure a smooth project kickoff."*

2. **Stakeholder Analysis**

   Prompt: *"How can we effectively identify and analyze project stakeholders? Share a stakeholder analysis template or framework."*

3. **Project Charter**

   Prompt: *"What should be included in a comprehensive project charter? Provide a template that covers all essential sections."*

4. **Work Breakdown Structure (WBS)**

   Prompt: *"How can we create a well-structured WBS? Share a step-by-step guide or WBS template for easy reference."*

5. **Project Schedule Development**

   Prompt: *"What are the best practices for developing a project schedule? Provide tips, techniques, and a sample schedule template."*

6. **Risk Register**

   Prompt: *"How can we effectively identify, assess, and manage project risks? Share a risk register template and guidelines for risk analysis."*

7. **Communication Plan**

   Prompt: *"What should be considered when developing a project communication plan? Provide a communication plan template and key communication channels."*

8. **Change Management**

   Prompt: *"How can we manage changes effectively? Share a change management process template and best practices."*

9. **Team Collaboration**

   Prompt: *"What are some effective tools and techniques for promoting team collaboration? Provide collaboration tips and collaboration platform recommendations."*

10. **Status Reporting**

    Prompt: *"How can we create concise and informative project status reports? Share a status report template and guidelines for reporting key metrics."*

11. **Issue Tracking & Resolution**

    Prompt: *"What is the recommended approach for tracking and resolving project issues? Provide an issue tracking template and guidelines for resolution."*

12. **Project Performance Monitoring**

    Prompt: *"How can we monitor project performance and track key metrics? Provide a project performance monitoring template and examples of essential metrics."*

13. **EVA Analysis**

    As the project manager, you are responsible for communicating the project's EVA analysis results to the stakeholders. Use this prompt to generate a comprehensive EVA analysis report that includes key metrics, performance analysis, and recommended corrective actions.

    Prompt: *"Provide a detailed EVA analysis report for the project stakeholders."*

    Input:

    Planned Value (PV): [Enter the planned value]

Earned Value (EV): [Enter the earned value]

Actual Cost (AC): [Enter the actual cost]

Output:

{EVA Analysis Report}

14. **Sprint Review (Scrum Master)**

Prompt: *"What are the key aspects to focus on during a sprint review? Provide a sprint review agenda template and tips for gathering valuable feedback."*

15. **Product Backlog Management (Product Owner)**

Prompt: *"How can the product backlog be managed effectively? Share a product backlog management template and techniques for backlog prioritization."*

16. **Retrospective Facilitation (Scrum Master)**

Prompt: *"What are some effective ways to facilitate retrospectives and drive continuous improvement? Provide a retrospective agenda template and tips for generating actionable insights."*

Here are 11 ready-to-use prompts for HR Sourcing Managers that cover the entire HR sourcing process, from job descriptions to job posting, leveraging social media for candidate sourcing, and using Boolean search operators for precise and targeted candidate searches:

1. Job Description Optimization: *"Optimize the job descriptions to attract the right candidates by highlighting key responsibilities, required skills, and qualifications."*

2. Job Posting Strategy: *"Design a job posting strategy that includes identifying the most effective job boards and platforms to reach the target talent pool."*

3. Social Media Candidate Sourcing: *"Leverage social media platforms, such as LinkedIn, Facebook, and Twitter to identify and engage with potential candidates who match the job requirements."*

4. Social Media Employer Branding: *"Develop an employer branding strategy on social media platforms to showcase the company culture, values, and opportunities to attract passive candidates."*

5. Boolean Search Operators: *"Train the recruitment team on using Boolean search operators such as AND, OR, NOT, and parentheses to create more precise and targeted candidate searches on job boards and databases."*

6. Talent Pool Creation: *"Build a talent pool of potential candidates who have shown interest in the company in the past but were not selected, for future sourcing needs."*

7. Referral Program: *"Implement a referral program among employees to encourage them to refer qualified candidates from their network and incentivize successful referrals."*

8. Resume Screening and Shortlisting: *"Establish a streamlined process for resume screening and shortlisting of candidates based on job requirements, skills, and qualifications."*

9. Candidate Engagement: *"Develop strategies to engage with potential candidates through personalized emails, follow-ups, and social media interactions, to build a relationship and maintain their interest."*

10. Metrics and Reporting: *"Set up tracking and reporting mechanisms to measure the effectiveness of different sourcing strategies, such as job boards, social media, and referrals, and optimize the process based on data-driven insights."*

11. Diversity and Inclusion Recruitment: *"Design and implement a recruitment strategy that promotes diversity and inclusion by actively sourcing and engaging candidates from underrepresented groups, creating inclusive job postings, and using inclusive language in all recruitment communications."*

 Prompt Cookbook for Small Businesses

Tom & Diana run a small business offering landscape design services to customers in the Bay Area. They leverage social media platforms like Facebook and Instagram for marketing their services. In the next quarter, they will launch their campaigns on TikTok as well. Their Yelp ratings have gone down of late and are a source of major concern to them.

They can do with some help from ChatGPT as their friendly co-pilot.

Here are 12 awesome ChatGPT prompts that small businesses like Tom & Diana's can use without much knowledge of prompt engineering to generate engaging and relevant responses:

1. *"Help me brainstorm creative marketing ideas for my small business to attract more customers."*

2. *"Suggest some strategies to boost my online presence and drive more traffic to my website."*

3. *"Write a compelling Facebook ad copy to drive traffic to our website and increase conversions."*

4. *"Write a catchy TikTok caption and hashtags for our product/service to increase visibility and engagement. "*

5. *"Provide tips on how to effectively use social media for promoting my small business and engaging with customers."*

6. *"Assist me in developing a compelling elevator pitch to communicate the value of my products/services to potential customers."*

7. *"Recommend some cost-effective ways to improve my customer service and enhance customer satisfaction."*

8. *"Give me ideas for unique and memorable promotions or events to create buzz and generate excitement for my small business."*

9. *"Help me optimize my website for better search engine rankings and increased visibility online."*

10. *"Suggest some creative collaborations or partnerships with other local businesses to mutually benefit and attract more customers."*

11. *"Provide insights on how to effectively use customer feedback to improve my products/services and build customer loyalty."*

12. *"Assist me in developing a content marketing strategy to share valuable and relevant content that resonates with my target audience and drives engagement."*

These prompts can help small businesses generate valuable ideas, insights, and strategies to enhance their marketing efforts, improve customer engagement, and drive business growth, without requiring extensive knowledge of prompt engineering or technical expertise.

Overview of Key Terms

1. **ChatGPT**: A large language model (LLM) developed by OpenAI that is capable of generating human-like text responses based on prompts provided to it.

2. **Prompt Engineering**: The process of designing and refining prompts to effectively guide the behavior of AI models like ChatGPT, in order to obtain desired outputs.

3. **Large Language Models**: Advanced AI models that are trained on vast amounts of text data to generate human-like text responses by predicting the most probable next word or phrase.

4. **Generative AI**: Generative AI refers to the field of artificial intelligence that focuses on autonomous or human-assisted systems that can generate new content, such as text, images, videos, and more. These systems use large datasets to learn and create content that is original and creative, often surpassing traditional rule-based systems.

5. **Transformer**: A type of neural network that is commonly used for generative AI tasks.

6. **Output Formats of GPT**: The different ways in which the generated text responses can be presented, such as single-sentence responses, multi-turn conversations, or system messages.

7. **Monetizing ChatGPT**: Strategies and approaches for leveraging ChatGPT to generate revenue or achieve financial gains, such as using it for content creation, customer service, or other business purposes.

8. **Clarity:** The quality of crafting clear and unambiguous prompts that effectively communicate the desired input or instruction to the AI model.

9. **Context**: Relevant information that is included in a prompt; incorporating relevant contextual information prompts to ensure that the AI model understands the user's need, intent, and the meaning behind the input.

10. **Precision**: Formulating prompts with accuracy and specificity to guide the AI model's behavior and obtain accurate and specific outputs.

11. **Sensitivity**: Being mindful of biases and ethical considerations in prompts to ensure that the AI model's responses are unbiased, fair, and aligned with ethical principles.

12. **Creativity**: Utilizing creativity in crafting prompts to generate engaging and diverse outputs from the AI model.

13. **Multi-turn Conversations**: Prompt engineering technique for designing prompts that facilitate multi-turn conversations, where the AI model responds in a contextually relevant manner based on previous interactions.

14. **System Messages**: System-targeted messages in prompts to guide the behavior of the AI model and provide context for users in interactive conversations.

15. **Prompt Engineering with Constraints**: Technique for incorporating constraints or limitations in prompts to guide the AI model's behavior within predefined boundaries or guidelines.

16. **Template-Based Forms**: Prompt engineering approach that utilizes template-based prompts to guide the AI model's responses in filling out forms or providing structured information.

17. **Prompt Engineering with Reward Models**: Technique that uses reinforcement learning and reward models to fine-tune the AI model's behavior and obtain desired outputs.

18. **Data Augmentation**: Artificially creating new variations of existing data, such as images or text, by applying modifications like rotation, scaling, or flipping. This helps increase the diversity and size of the data used for training machine learning models.

19. **Best Practices in Prompt Engineering**: Guidelines and recommendations for effectively designing prompts, testing and iterating them, incorporating feedback from AI models, and ensuring optimal performance.

20. **ChatGPT API**: Overview of the ChatGPT-specific Application Programming Interface (API), which is a set of protocols and tools used to build software applications and enable communication between different systems or applications. The discussion includes ChatGPT APIs' functionalities, methods of interaction, and tips for effective utilization in real-world scenarios.

21. **Challenges in Prompt Engineering**: Common challenges and pitfalls in prompt engineering, such as addressing biases, ensuring accuracy, and managing user expectations.

22. **Ethical Considerations**: Discussing the ethical implications of prompt engineering, including biases, fairness, privacy, and responsible use of AI technologies.

23. **One-Shot Prompt**: In a single prompt, the AI model is given all the information needed to generate a complete response.

24. **Multi-Turn Prompt**: Multiple prompts are provided to the AI model in a sequence, with each prompt building on the previous one to generate a complete response.

25. **Conditional Prompt**: A type of prompt that includes a conditional statement or constraint that the AI model must follow when generating a response.

26. **Contextual Prompt**: A type of prompt that provides context for the AI model to generate a response. The context can include information about the user, the topic, or the conversation history.

27. **Generative Prompt**: A type of prompt that allows the AI model to generate responses freely, without any specific constraints or guidelines.

28. **Prompt Expansion**: A technique in which a single prompt is expanded into multiple related prompts, allowing the AI model to generate more varied and diverse responses.

29. **Prompt Chaining**: A technique in which the output of one prompt is used as the input for the next prompt, allowing the AI model to generate a longer and more coherent response.

30. **Cheat Sheets**: Quick reference guides including ready-to-use templates for different roles, such as content marketers, marketing managers, product managers, and HR sourcing managers, providing practical examples and tips for leveraging prompt engineering in their specific domains.

Supplemental Learning Content

Learning has to be a continual activity to stay ahead of the curve. No single book can cover adequately all the pieces of the puzzle, especially in a nascent area like Generative AI where we are at a pivotal moment and things are just beginning to unfold. A year in the field of AI is akin to what happens in most other industries over a period of a decade or more.

I have created a companion website for this book at www.getAIready.com to provide you with supplemental information on related topics that can enhance your learning and deliver additional value to the book reader. Feel free to browse this site regularly for engaging blog content, tips and insights and any downloads available on the site.

Thank You.

Harish Bhat